"The Gospel needs to be p.
This book serves as a catalyst _____
engaging and relatable storie. _____
mative power of the Gospel like no other book I've read.

–Beau Eckert, senior pastor at Calvary Church

"The beauty, the power, and the simplicity of the Gospel knows no cultural bounds. Wherever it reaches around the world, it is a beacon of light, and it redeems those who are broken beyond human repair. Daniel takes us to the heart—to the truth of stories about people who experience unbelievable suffering and yet find hope. This book paints a picture of the power of the Gospel."

–Anne Beiler, founder of Auntie Anne's Pretzels

"I found *#Gospel* incredibly engaging. It is a well-written interaction over the meaning of the Gospel from the book of Romans, applied with real-life stories and illustrations. I especially enjoyed Daniel's short, but thought-provoking segments from history and daily life. You will enjoy this book!"

–Barry Wissler, president of HarvestNET International

"In a culture where words like 'gospel' are rapidly losing their meaning, Daniel gives us a loving and thoughtful reminder that the Gospel of Jesus is anything but meaningless. It is *the* story—the one that binds all the rest of them together."

–Andrew Peterson, singer and songwriter,
author of *The Wingfeather Saga*

"Have you ever wanted to see the deeper concepts and themes of the Gospel laid out in today's language? How about clear examples and analogies that are applicable to the culture today? *#Gospel* spells out the Good News of Jesus, walking its readers through Romans with ease and excitement. It masterfully balances and explains the hard-to-grasp concepts. I'd encourage both seekers and believers to open this book. It's for anyone wanting to see the facts, validity, and relevance found in the Gospel message. Daniel doesn't leave questions unanswered as he points us to the main answer Himself: Jesus Christ."

–Joel Bomberger, *Circuit Riders* evangelist

"In a world that is increasingly noisy and complex, Daniel brilliantly simplifies the message of God's redeeming love made available for every person in a way that this generation can understand. Through stories from scripture, *#Gospel* shows how God's love intersects with real life. It is a must-read!"

–Matt Mylin, lead pastor of the Worship Center

"Deep in the heart of each of us is a longing to know the answers to the questions, 'God, are You really there? What do You think of me? Can I really know You?' In this book, Daniel will take you on a journey to find the answers to these questions. And the answers are better than you could ever hope! The story he invites you into is true to the gospel, engaging, and personal. You'll be glad you took him up on his invitation to journey toward the heart of God."

–Scott Arbeiter, president of World Relief

#GOSPEL

Life, Hope, and Truth for Generation Now

Daniel Rice

SHILOH RUN  PRESS
An Imprint of Barbour Publishing, Inc.

Foreword

Many of the most significant conversations in my life have occurred around the table.

It was over cabbage stew in Moscow that I learned about microenterprise development, a conversation which would forever alter the trajectory of my life. I proposed to the woman who would one day become my wife over a hollowed-out pineapple filled with stir fry. My job offer at HOPE International was accompanied by a steaming plate of Chicken Tikka Masala.

Given that food seems to hallmark my most pivotal moments, perhaps it shouldn't be surprising that it was over an Aussie burger that I first met Daniel Rice. At the onset of our meal together, Daniel confidently proclaimed that as far as burgers went, the Aussie burger was unrivaled. Reading through the description, I remained unconvinced. After all, what kind of burger includes grilled pineapple, pickled beets, smoked Gouda, and a fried egg?

As it turns out, Daniel was right. The unconventional burger remains to this day, the very best that I've ever had.

As remarkable as that burger was, it was our conversation that day that left the most lasting impression.

It didn't take long to come to understand that Daniel's heart beats for Christ's fame and glory both in his own life and across the globe. He exemplifies wholehearted, relentless pursuit of Christ—and longs to make Him known. Daniel is a man whose heart has been irrevocably captured by the grace of God, and the Lord's work in his life has left an indelible mark on my own.

I'll never forget the grief in Daniel's eyes as he shared the stories of friends who had never truly understood the captivating message of grace in Christ. Something in him seemed to come alive as he shared about his passion to take the timeless truths of Scripture and teach them in a way that a modern audience could better understand. It was clear that #Gospel was so much more than a book he wanted to write—it was a calling he felt compelled by God to answer.

Our lunch that day was the start of a lifelong friendship with someone I deeply appreciate, greatly admire, and constantly learn from. Daniel is someone I seek out for counsel before making important decisions, and during my most painful moments over recent years, he has spoken gospel-saturated words of hope and encouragement. He masterfully weaves wisdom and compassion together in a way that I personally long to more fully grasp.

The apostle Paul wrote, "Follow my example, as I follow the example of Christ" (1 Corinthians 11:1 NIV). Although he would feel uncomfortable with it, I know that when I follow Daniel's example, I come closer to following Christ. It is with great joy that I commend him to you as a trusted guide in your own faith journey.

In the pages of this book, you will hear the "old, old story" in a fresh, new way. Through innovative storytelling and unexpected connections, Daniel takes the timeless, radical truths of the gospel and reframes them for today's audience—and in so doing, helps us to better understand how even our most ordinary, mundane moments connect to the greatest story the world will ever know.

My hope is that this wouldn't simply be a book that you read, but rather a discussion that you enter into. I pray that these themes of wild grace and restoration would become inextricably woven into the fabric of your life. As Daniel connects the gospel to the most unconventional stories, I pray that you would begin to connect it to your own stories as you trace God's goodness and faithfulness in your own life. In Deuteronomy 11:19, the Israelites are commanded to tell and retell the stories of God's goodness and faithfulness to them. They're told to "teach them to your children, talking about them when you sit at home and when you walk along the road, when you lie down and when you get up." May #Gospel serve as a helpful tool in your own storytelling.

What you hold in your hands is far more than just a book. You're holding an invitation to enter into the most important conversation this world will ever have about the greatest rescue the world has ever seen. It's a conversation about a redeeming God of unstoppable love who is relentless in His passionate pursuit of you. It's a conversation that will change your life, if you'll let it.

Welcome to *#Gospel*.

Peter Greer,
President & CEO, HOPE International

Introduction

Five to ten seconds.

After that, the filter kicks in.

In our day and age, five to ten seconds is usually all the time we're given to persuade someone that what we have to say is worthy of his or her time. You and I live in a world suffering from a relentless bombardment of information. Television, social media, advertising, acquaintances, friends, and family all vie for time and an attentive ear. *Is it relevant to me?* Without realizing it, we ask ourselves this question countless times throughout the day. *Do I want what this advertiser is selling? Will this be on the test? Is this conversation significant to my situation? Will this news affect my life at all?* If we don't adapt and learn to filter out what does not apply to us, we quickly become overwhelmed. In this new world of burst communication, our presentation of this Gospel needs to be adapted as well. This is the aim of *#Gospel*.

A hashtag (#) is a symbol used on social media to mark and group messages related to a specific topic. Since these messages are by nature open for everyone to see, hash-tagging a term invites others to join an open conversation and adds the author's thoughts to our modern-day global exchange of ideas. This is the heart of *#Gospel*. This book is designed to be an open conversation, using current cultural references and stories to draw us into a thoughtful dialogue about what the Gospel really is and how it radically alters our everyday lives. *#Gospel* is not a ground-breaking collection of new ideas; it simply breaks down Paul's explanation of the Gospel in Romans in a way that is accessible and engaging for culture today. It is my hope that this book will bring new life to the ancient truth that is still every bit as relevant today as it was two thousand years ago. I pray that it gives fresh life and hope to those who have felt burned by and detached from the religion they were raised in, helpful illumination for those who have always been curious about spiritual things they observed but were never really connected with, and a new perspective for those who are doing their best to daily follow the teachings of Jesus.

Welcome to the conversation.

Chapter 1
#CoffeeTalk

Measure for me the abyss of man's wickedness and guilt during all the ages of his black and hateful history, that I may realize in some degree what that world is which God has loved; and then, pausing for a moment in wonder at the thought that such a world could be loved at all, hasten to speak of love that gave the Son.

—Sir Robert Anderson

Whoever said love makes the world go 'round clearly had never heard about coffee. The amount of money people will happily fork over for what in essence is just heated bean water is staggering. The United States alone spent $18 billion on coffee beverages last year.[1] No longer is it simply a hot cuppa purchased every morning from the local diner. There are now entire, wildly successful business models built on the back of the modest Arabica bean. In some places, people are even defined by the coffee that they drink. Many go to great lengths in pursuit of the

---

1. "Coffee Drinking Statistics," Statisticsbrain.com, accessed July 19, 2017, http://www.statisticbrain.com/coffee-drinking-statistics/.

perfect cup. Even home coffee brewers aren't what they used to be. Instead of the glass pot drip coffee makers and stove-top percolators of yesteryear, we're now infatuated by the Keurig.

Coffee is an enormous part of life and culture all over the world. From the twenty-four-hour diner to the local gourmet coffee hipster joint, this energy-giving elixir has asserted itself into almost every part of our daily lives. Some people depend on its potency to propel them from their pillows into their workday. For others, each sip is a calming, almost ritualistic retreat from the stress and pressure of the busy day. Coffee serves as the great equalizer. World leaders from the most powerful nations in the world drink it. Astronauts drink it. Garbage collectors, museum curators, subway train operators, heart surgeons, and the people who stuff takeout Chinese menus under your windshield wiper drink it as well. Coffee is a worldwide phenomenon.

Given that the experience of a cup of coffee is almost universal, let's compare it to people. Let's say that the good and noble things that people do with their lives represent the quality of a cup of coffee. Someone we would call morally upright or selfless, like Gandhi or Mother Teresa, would be an impeccable cup of pour-over coffee. Every culture has these paragons of virtue, the heroes we long for our children to grow up to emulate. We aren't simply talking about good coffee; this is the stuff of legend. To obtain this kind of coffee would require the rental of a private jet to fly into the heart of the mountains of Columbia to collect the finest beans available, picked by the hands of Juan Valdez himself, and then to return that very day to maintain peak freshness. The beans would then need to be roasted, rested, and ground to perfection by a world champion barista. Coffee of this caliber would then require a second jet to be dispatched to gather crystal clear, icy spring water from an aquifer deep within the pristine, protected Canadian wilderness. These two elements would then be combined flawlessly in the brewing process at precisely the right temperature before being poured carefully into a priceless artifact, taken from the collection of Louis XIV himself, crafted from the finest china and hand-gilded with twenty-four-karat gold. Indeed, that would be the finest (and most outlandish!) cup of coffee the world has ever seen! On the other hand, a person most of us would consider harmful to society might be represented by a suspect pot of coffee from a dirty gas station, probably brewed and burned before you were born. This pot has been sitting out for so long that when poured into the crusty paper cup on hand, it has the murky consistency of old motor oil. It tastes like the bottom of a zookeeper's boot. We set these two wildly different cups on opposite ends of an endless table, with every other conceivable type of coffee stretched out between them. Coffee from Starbucks, Tim Horton's, Dunkin Donuts, and representatives from every conceivable gourmet shop and cafe are lined up next to brews from gas stations and fast food chains. Now, suppose that after we do this, in through the door walks a somber-looking man in a spotless white lab coat. He is carrying a stainless steel briefcase, out of which he pulls a small glass vial labeled CYANIDE. If you are not familiar with cyanide, it is a toxin among the fastest lethal poisons known to humankind. Cyanide causes death within minutes to hours of exposure. The man proceeds to slowly remove the vial's lid, before painstakingly placing a single drop of the solution into every single coffee cup. He carefully returns the now-empty vial to his shiny briefcase and asks politely, "Which cup of coffee would you like to drink?" It is, of course, a foolish question. No matter how lowly or grand the cup of coffee might have been before the poison, it has all been corrupted. No one would choose to drink any of the coffee if he or she accurately understood the consequences of doing so.

This is the story of Romans 1 in distilled form. In these first few verses, Paul outlines a similar picture of the human condition. No matter who you are, great or small, man or woman, famous or infamous, all of us have been born with a deadly contaminant: sin. Sin is our failure to hit the mark of perfection. No matter how noble a person's actions are, no matter how much he or she works toward the greater good, no matter how spectacular his or her "coffee" offering, nothing can eliminate the toxin of sin. Your skin color, social status, and sexual orientation have no bearing here. No amount of talent or charisma can tip the scale. The playing field is leveled. All sin is lethal, and no one escapes its deadly effect. Everyone starts from precisely the same place. There are no classes or tiered ranks of acceptability. This is the foundation for the Gospel.

It is with this good news in mind that Paul opens his letter to the Romans with the following words in verses 16–17 of the first chapter:

> *For I am not ashamed of this Good News about Christ. It is the power of God at work, saving everyone who believes—the Jew first and also the Gentile. This Good News tells us how God makes us right in his sight. This is accomplished from start to finish by faith. As the Scriptures say, "It is through faith that a righteous person has life." (NLT)*

As he penned these words, one can only imagine the passion that flowed from his quill, tempered by years of suffering and pain for the sake of the one he labored for. He had forsaken his former life and set out on a journey to take this Gospel to the ends of his world. Paul was all in.

#UnlikelyActivist

Born with the name Saul, in one of the largest trade centers on the Mediterranean coast, Paul most likely received his second name through his father, a Roman citizen. The name *Paul* was Latin, and it was very common for Jews of that day to have two names: one Hebrew, the other Latin or Greek.[2] Saul's family was a deeply religious family that was wealthy enough to send their son to Jerusalem to receive his education at the prestigious school of a Pharisee named Gamaliel, one of the most notable rabbis in recorded history. In Jedi terms, Gamaliel was to a young Saul what Obi-wan was to Luke Skywalker. His school was renowned for providing students with a balanced education, and it is probable that Paul had broad exposure to classical literature, philosophy, and ethics.[3] Interestingly, it was Master Gamaliel who would later come to the defense of a budding new movement seen as an enormous threat to the religious establishment of the day, led by a ragtag band of common fisherman, tradesmen, a revolutionary, and a tax collector. Having been molded in a cocoon of strict adherence to the Law, Paul's hatred for this new movement began to simmer. He was present as the

---

2. Ferdinand Prat, "St. Paul." In *The Catholic Encyclopedia*. vol. 11. (New York: Robert Appleton Company, 1911).

3. Quency E. Wallace, "The Early Life and Background of Paul the Apostle," *The American Journal of Biblical Theology*, (2002).

pious kingpins of his order crushed the life out of one of the new upstarts named Stephen with stones, and his thirst for blood only grew. Soon Paul would become a leader in the fight to scour this new sect from the face of the earth. His gruesome exploits earned him the fear of many, and even after his dramatic transformation, it would take time and the help of a brave advocate for the heads of this new faction of Christ followers to trust him.

It was a quest for blood and justice that propelled Paul to start out on a journey that would forever alter the course of his life. He set out for Damascus, determined to capture and kill any who associated with the Way. His trip took an unexpected turn when he came face-to-face with the very God he believed he was defending and finally came to understand that the origin of this new sect, Jesus Christ, was exactly who He said He was. He was instructed to go see a man in Damascus named Ananias, and though his encounter left him blind, he did just that.

Due to Paul's fearsome reputation, Ananias was none too happy to hear of his arrival. Ananias had likely personally known some of the victims of Paul's homicidal raging. After arguing his point with God Himself, Ananias eventually relented and set out to meet the monster responsible for so much death and suffering of the believers in Jerusalem. Paul remained in Damascus for several days and immediately began preaching in the Jewish synagogues that Jesus Christ was God. This was such an about-face that people who heard about it were completely dumbfounded. After all, this was the same man who had come to Damascus to crush the very idea that he was now preaching as truth! The local religious leaders were so angry that they plotted to kill Paul, and his new friends had to concoct a crazy escape plan to smuggle him out of the city. What was it about this message that was so important, so radical, so powerful and revolutionary that it could change its greatest persecutor into such a wholehearted ally? What was it about this Gospel that was so divisive that it became a death sentence for those fearless enough to broadcast it publicly?

#FrozenCure

The word *Gospel* literally means "good news." In an inescapable disaster, this is the message that turns the tide. In 2014, there was a particularly virulent outbreak of the Ebola virus in a few countries in Africa. Ebola is almost always deadly and has claimed millions of lives over the years. A few brave medical doctors and workers were courageous enough to travel to the heart of the outbreak to treat the victims—a valiant, incredibly dangerous endeavor. Soon enough, some of them were infected, and one soon died. Two of the infected were American missionaries named Nancy Writebol and Dr. Kent Brantly. Nine days after Brantly was infected, his condition had deteriorated rapidly. His breathing was labored, and he knew that he was dying. Kent called his wife and two young children in the United States to say good-bye. One can only imagine the crushing agony his wife experienced as she listened to her husband's labored breathing over the phone. In that moment of desperation, something remarkable happened. An experimental serum was flown in by a small pharmaceutical company based in San Diego. The serum had never been tested on humans, but it offered the very thing Kent needed: hope. He was snatched from the very jaws of death, and within hours of administration, the vaccine had completely reversed the course of the deadly disease ravaging Kent's body. The phone call home to his wife with this "good news" must have been breathtaking to hear. Rescued from certain death, both Brantly and Writebol had been given a new chance at life.[4] Hope when all seems lost. Good news in an impossible situation. From death to life—this is the story of the Gospel.

4. Sanjay Gupta and Danielle Dellorto, "Experimental Drug Likely Saved Ebola Patients," CNN.com, August 5, 2014, http://www.cnn.com/2014/08/04/health/experimental-ebola-serum/index.html?iid=article_sidebar.

#FrozenHeart

In 2013, Disney released an animated film that would obliterate all previous box office records set by movies in its genre. It was a colossal success by any standard and raked in over $1.3 billion worldwide. I know this well, because I have three young daughters. Like most little girls, they were *Frozen* fanatics. The story was an interesting one. The characters were well developed, and the artwork was extraordinary. In some ways it was the typical Disney fare, princesses and villains, comical little side characters, and lots of conversational singing, but something about this particular story stood out to me. The more I saw it, the more I couldn't unsee it: a picture of the human condition. Warning, spoilers are ahead if you are one of the last remaining inhabitants of planet earth who hasn't seen this movie. *Frozen* is a love story, but not in the way that one might expect. The tale unfolds as two sisters, Elsa and Anna, are emotionally driven apart by a childhood accident, some unfortunate parenting, and a mysterious secret. Elsa has the magical ability to control ice and snow, and while playing with Anna one night, she almost accidentally kills her. Her parents, fearful for Anna's safety, forbid any further contact between the sisters, which leads to incredible loneliness and confusion. The problem is exacerbated when their parents are lost at sea, leaving each of them very much alone. On Elsa's coronation day, throngs of people gather to celebrate her crowning, including a prince from a neighboring kingdom named Hans. Anna and Hans hit it off right away and seem to be the perfect match, but when they tell Elsa, she disagrees. An argument ensues, and Elsa loses control of her powers, shattering the celebration with shards of ice before bolting off into the frigid night, with Anna in close pursuit. As the story unfolds, Anna is once again unintentionally struck by her sister's ice magic, and we find out in true fairy tale fashion that only an act of true love can save her. She rushes back to Hans, hoping that a kiss from him will break the spell, but it becomes increasingly clear that Hans has no love for her and is secretly plotting to overthrow the kingdom. In the climax of the movie, Hans raises his sword to cut Elsa down, but in an act of "true love," Anna throws herself in front of the blade, choosing to sacrifice her life for her sister instead of running into the arms of the man she's fallen in love with. What struck me was the crystal-clear portrayal of the two sides of the human heart: selfishness and love. All of our actions stem from one of these two motivations— from the time we enter this world, a writhing mass of dependency and helplessness, to our proudest, most accomplished moments. Once, Jesus was asked what the most important command of God was. His answer was simple: love. Love God. Love others. If God is a truly perfect and holy God, He must demand perfection from anyone in His presence. No one has ever been able to choose love over self every time. No one is perfect. Everyone has missed the mark. Everyone is contaminated by sin. Even an incredibly sacrificial act like Anna's is not enough if it has been marred by a less-than-perfect life. Jesus is our atoning sacrifice to God not simply because He gave His life for us but because He lived the perfect life that we were incapable of living and then traded our records for His.

In the end, we each have only two choices. We can choose selfishness, or we can choose self-sacrificing, unconditional, true love. The heart of the Gospel is news of how True Love defeated sin and death and rose again.

It was for this very reason that Paul was so passionate and unflinching about the Gospel in his life and writings. In that news, desperation and hope hung in the balance. In that news, the eternal condition of the human soul would be determined. In that news, life sprang out from jaws of death.

This is the Gospel. Hope for the hopeless. Humanity, once dead in sin, being made alive in Christ. Forgiveness for the unforgivable.

No one escapes the taint of sin. We are all infected. We desperately need a cure. The Gospel is the message we have all been waiting for.

Chapter 2
#That'sNotFair!

Whoever undertakes to set himself up as a judge of Truth and Knowledge is shipwrecked by the laughter of the gods.
—ALBERT EINSTEIN

Screen time is a big deal in my house. It is prized above all other things by my five wonderful children. Food, sleep, and interaction with other humans are all considered secondary priorities when compared to the wonders of the magical display on the iPad or computer. The trancelike state into which each of them falls while staring at a glowing screen is a sight to behold. To be honest, I'd imagine that some of the blame falls squarely on the shoulders of their father, who has a bit of a penchant for gaming himself. (But please don't mention this to their mother.) Enthralled by a world of epic battles, magical ponies, and resources waiting to be mined and crafted into great monuments to imagination and creativity, these little technophiles would happily sit glued to a screen all day long, if their loving and all-wise parental units didn't set firm limits in place on how much they are allowed to partake. It is easy to see, then, how a perceived inequality in the distribution of allotments for screen time could make for a catastrophic disaster.

Enter one eight-year-old boy, livid with frustration about the possibility of his older brother being allowed more time with the precious Holy Grail. I knew the words that were coming before they had even passed over his lips: "That's not fair!"

As people, we are obsessed with fairness, particularly for us and those we care about. When the guy driving the BMW rolls to a partial stop at the four-way and then guns it, knowing full well that it was your turn next, it's irritating. When the lines at the supermarket are crawling and your family is waiting for you to get home for dinner, and someone carrying an armload of items cuts the "Five Items or Less" line in front of you to join someone she knows, the nagging little voice inside you screams. When the position you have been working toward for years is filled by someone underqualified and undereducated simply because he or she is friends with the boss, it's hard to maintain your composure. Unfairness is all around us.

#UnavoidableSuffering

From mildly annoying to grotesquely terrifying, injustice on this planet is inescapable. Recently a young boy in Detroit was shot while sleeping in his bed by someone involved in a gang-related shootout on his street. He was a good kid who played Little League baseball and loved his family. As of yet, there are no suspects. Where is the fairness in this?

On July 17, 2014, a Boeing 777 with 298 people aboard was cruising through the air at 33,000 feet on a flight from Amsterdam to their destination in Kuala Lumpur. Completely unaware of the danger hurtling toward them, doctors, students, bankers, families en route to their vacations, and over 80 children would soon be casualties of one of the most horrific air disasters in history. Far below in the eastern mountains of Ukraine, rebels in a conflict with Kiev launched a radar-guided surface-to-air missile that rocketed toward the plane. Their lives were cut tragically short by violence; there were no survivors.[5,6] In the months that followed, there was plenty of finger pointing and righteous indignation, but no one was held accountable for the mass carnage.

Human suffering is all around us. Even the ones charged with meting out justice have often been unable to do so in a fair and impartial manner as we have seen from civil rights history and countless cases of abuse worldwide. The abject poverty of homeless children living on the streets of Brazil,

---

5. "MH17 Crash: Passengers On Malaysia Airlines Plane In Ukraine," BBC News, July 20, 2014, http://www.bbc.com/news/world-asia-28360827.

6. Cathering E. Sholchet and Ashley Fantz, "U.S. Official: Missile Shot Down Malaysia Airlines Plane," CNN.com, July 18, 2014, http://www.cnn.com/2014/07/17/world/europe/ukraine-malaysia-airlines-crash/index.html?hpt=hp_t1.

the unspeakable suffering of the vulnerable at the hands of genocidal dictators, and the horror of a world where women and children are bought and sold for sex are but a few of the heartrending examples of the brokenness that pervades our planet. In his bestselling book *The Locust Effect*, director of the International Justice Mission Gary Haugen details a few of these crushing stories in their severity.[7] In one, an eight-year-old girl named Yuri is brutally raped and murdered in a small Peruvian village, her body thrown out into the street and abandoned by her tormentors. When her blood and clothing are found in the home of a rich and influential townsperson, it becomes undeniably clear who the perpetrators are. When Yuri's heartbroken parents plead with the local authorities for justice, they are obstructed at every turn. Evidence is destroyed. Requests for transparency are denied. Even the town prosecutor refuses the case based on the lack of ability for the grieving family to pay for his services. When the very system set in place to protect the vulnerable works only for the ones oppressing them, chaos and despair abound.

Every government system is flawed. The problem lies not with the systems themselves but with the people charged to run them. Capitalism is marred by the inevitable corruption that greed and materialism bring. Both socialism and communism would theoretically solve the

---

7. Gary A. Haugen, *The Locust Effect* (New York, NY: Oxford University Press 2014), 4.

societal problems of poverty and crime if the citizenry were by nature always moral, hardworking, and selfless—but that is never the case for long. There are no incorruptible systems, only ways to fight or delay corruption. However, when those tasked with fighting the corruption become corrupt themselves, everything begins to crumble.

Where is the fairness here?

Where is the justice?

#FlawedJustice

If these are the questions you ask when you hear stories of injustice, you are not alone. The longing for equality is something that resonates in every heart, transcending ethnicity or creed. We all yearn for someone to set things right. The systems of justice on which we depend here on earth are often ineffective, corrupted, and broken. That brokenness has been put on display through the Innocence Project, an organization dedicated to exonerating wrongly convicted people through the use of DNA testing. To date, the project has led to the freeing of 316 wrongfully convicted people, including eighteen who spent time on death row.

Put yourself in the shoes of a court justice. Day after day, docket after docket, you are responsible for determining the truth in situations where deception and evasion are almost a certainty. Case after case, the ugly side of man's struggle for power and wealth are showcased in gruesome detail. You weren't at the scene of the alleged crime and must rely on the testimony of others and interpret the evidence presented to you. People are prone to forget or lie, and facts can be construed and manipulated in a myriad of different ways. How do you determine the innocent from the guilty? Is innocence really just a matter of how much one can afford to pay for a defense attorney? Is guilt merely the inability to do so? Even if a judge had the ability to be at every crime scene the moment the act in question had taken place, all issues are not resolved. To accurately mete out justice, a judge must be able to clearly discern the intent of a person's heart.

I am a recovering trypanophobe. Now while that sounds bad, it's actually an overly elaborate way to describe a fairly common condition: the immense, almost uncontrollable fear of needles. When I was a kid, I used to hate going to the dentist or doctor's office for one reason: I didn't like the idea of someone stabbing me with a sharp metal object. It is estimated that at least 10 percent of American adults suffer from a fear of needles, and it is likely that the actual number is even larger, as the most severe cases are never documented due to the tendency of the sufferer to avoid all medical treatment.[8] Now, there

---

8. James G. Hamilton, "Needle Phobia—A Neglected Diagnosis," *Journal of Family Practice* 41, no. 2 (1995): 169–175.

is an enormous difference between getting stabbed and getting a flu shot, but in the mind of a six-year-old boy with an aversion to needles, they can seem pretty similar. What, then, is the primary difference between the two? I would suggest that it is intent.

Intent is the inner motivation that compels us to act. It is the reason behind the response. Intent changes everything. It is the difference between surgery and mutilation, between involuntary manslaughter and capital murder, between twelve months in prison and death row.

Even if a judge were able to be present at every single crime ever committed, determining the intent of the human heart is a tricky task. Some are better at masking it than others. A judge that can deliver perfect justice would have to be able to perfectly see into the depths of the human soul to accurately discern the truth.

#TheHeroWeDeserve

In 2008, Christopher Nolan continued his retelling of the classic tale of a crime-fighting vigilante pitted against the forces of evil in a struggle for the future of the city of Gotham. One man, against all odds, fights for truth and justice in a world of chaotic evil, greed, and corruption. Bruce Wayne has seemingly limitless resources, a brilliant mind, a well-trained and battle-hardened physique, and an unbreakable will. The Dark Knight is a beacon of hope in a city overrun by darkness. Isn't a superhero precisely what we need in real life?

Most comic book superheroes have powers related to their size, strength, speed, or skill. They control their surroundings by harnessing a strange power or blast through obstacles with sheer force. In all of his fictional glory, Batman still falls far short of the hero we need. One man cannot see the actions of all or hope to know their hearts or motives. Power corrupts, and the constant barrage of depravity can desensitize even the most compassionate heart.

In the end, we need a hero that doesn't exist. We desperately need an impartial judge, incorruptible, and perfect in all ways. This seems like an impossible request. Even if such a judge existed, the necessary qualifications are unattainable. They are unreachable, that is, for everyone except One.

The finite cannot fully contain the Infinite. In the next few moments, we are going to examine some aspects of the infinite that God has revealed to us. Many a well-meaning theologian or scholar has become bogged down in the deep morass of systematic theology and the finer points of academic spirituality, classifying and codifying the nature and attributes of God. Some have become so entangled in the minutia of manmade doctrine and spiritual debate about the gray areas and unknowns of God's infinite character that they forget about one very important thing: God knows us and wants us to know Him. To that end, He has provided His Word to make clear some very specific things that He wants us to know. Here are four things God has revealed about Himself in His Word that make Him the perfect candidate to be our final judge:

1. He is omnipresent—present everywhere. The concept is a difficult one to wrap our minds around, but the authors of Scripture repeatedly speak of this aspect of God's character:

> *Can a man hide himself in secret places so that I cannot see him? declares the LORD. Do I not fill heaven and earth? declares the LORD. (Jeremiah 23:24 ESV)*

> *The eyes of the LORD are in every place, keeping watch on the evil and the good. (Proverbs 15:3 ESV)*

> *Where shall I go from your Spirit? Or where shall I flee from your presence? If I ascend to heaven, you are there! If I make my bed in Sheol, you are there! If I take the wings of the morning and dwell in the uttermost parts of the sea, even there your hand shall lead me, and your right hand shall hold me. (Psalm 139:7–10 ESV)*

> *And no creature is hidden from his sight, but all are naked and exposed to the eyes of him to whom we*

must give account. (Hebrews 4:13 ESV)

There is no place that God does not see. There is nothing anyone has ever done or ever will do that He has not witnessed. There are no bad camera angles, no grainy footage, and no blurry images with the Almighty. There is no angelic CSI unit scurrying around the universe to collect evidence to solve cases, although that might make for a pretty entertaining spinoff. God is present everywhere, and nothing is hidden from Him.

2. He is omniscient—all knowing. Humankind has an almost unquenchable thirst for knowledge. The more we learn, the more we understand how little we actually know about the universe we live in and the way that it operates. Each new discovery only serves to expose new mysteries waiting to be understood, but for our Infinite Creator, the knowledge is already His.

For whenever our heart condemns us, God is greater than our heart, and he knows everything. (1 John 3:20 ESV)

Have you not known? Have you not heard? The LORD is the everlasting God, the Creator of the ends of the earth. He does not faint or grow weary; his understanding is unsearchable. (Isaiah 40:28 ESV)

We spend incredible amounts of money in the pursuit of knowledge. The right information at the right time can equate to an enormous payoff in the financial industry. According to the St. Louis Federal Reserve Bank, the total amount of student loan debt outstanding has grown from $509 billion in 2006 to $1.31 trillion as of the third quarter of 2014.[9] In the world of international espionage, massive resources, even human lives, are dedicated to countries vying for critical information on the weaknesses and strengths of both their friends and enemies. In all this relentless pursuit of knowledge, even the best education, connections, and experience can't provide the tools needed to understand the motives of the human heart.

Sean Spencer and Burton Guster were two characters from one of my favorite television series, Psych. Sean, who is a fake psychic, has been trained by his father, a retired police officer, to be incredibly observant. He and his reluctant partner, Gus, solve crimes by convincing people that Sean can read minds, but in reality, they are merely savvy detectives with a love for pop culture and pineapple. However, in order to accurately mete out justice, this ability to "read minds" can't simply be a fictional skill in a TV show. The ability to discern the difference between premeditated murder and involuntary manslaughter is essential to accuracy in judgment, and God's ability goes so much further than mind reading. He knows thoughts before they

---

9. Todd Campbell, "The Average American Owes This Much In Student Loan Debt—How Do You Compare?" The Motley Fool, January 24, 2015, http://www.fool.com/investing/general/2015/01/24/the-average-american-owes-this-much-in-student-loa.aspx.

are formed, actions before they are done, and motives before they are acted upon.

3. He is all powerful. The ability to see a problem and the capability to remedy it are very different things. Many people have decried systemic racism over the last century, but few have been able to curtail its ugly effects. The God who spoke the universe into existence and formed galaxies we haven't even discovered yet, who goes before all things and holds all things together, is the one Being with enough power to make things right. There is no jurisdiction that is outside His reach.

4. Finally, and possibly most importantly of all, God is incorruptible. Humans are motivated by many things. The siren songs of wealth, fame, romance, and power have lured many of history's most notable figures to the dark side. We want what we don't have, and given the chance, we will often stop at nothing to get it—at the peril of our very souls. Each of us has his or her own Achilles' heel.

Thelma grew up in a city not far from where I live. Her parents were religious, educated, and nurturing—and they adored her. Thelma attended a prestigious private Catholic school and graduated from Temple University with a degree in real estate management. She possessed all the tools that our culture deems necessary to live a happy, successful life, but still, she felt that something was missing. Thelma found that "something" driving a striking red convertible down the street one hot summer day in 1977. His name was Jackie, and he was everything that she thought she wanted. She was drawn to his charisma, his extravagant style, and the respect he commanded as part of the Black Mafia—a ruthless gang of drug dealers known for killing police officers. No one forced Thelma into a relationship with Jackie, but the tantalizing lure of what he offered was irresistible to her. They had a son together, and for a time, their lives looked idyllic. Unfortunately, Thelma's dream turned into a nightmare when Jackie was found rolled up in a carpet with a fatal gunshot wound to the head. Thelma quickly assumed control of her late husband's illicit drug operation and began to expand rapidly. Her organization grew so large that in the early 1990s it ran from Los Angeles to Philadelphia. Thelma quickly earned the nicknames "Boss Lady" and "Queen Pen" and earned an estimated $400,000 in profit every month.[10] What would cause someone to leave behind a promising future and join an occupation that throws lives away like yesterday's garbage? Why would anyone choose to raise a son in such a dangerous environment? The answer is simple: for the same reason powerful political leaders all over the world choose to throw away their integrity for the promise of more wealth or power. It's the same reason high school students are pressured

10. "Thelma Wright," Biography.com, accessed July 19, 2017, http://www
.biography.com/people/thelma-wright-21241567.

into taking part in things they would never otherwise do to gain that coveted status of acceptance. It's the same reason the one whose responsibility it is to defend the vulnerable and protect the defenseless turns his head while the helpless are oppressed and exploited by the ones rich enough to bribe him. Corruption is all about selfishly filling a desire at any cost.

The Creator stands alone in His incorruptibility. There is nothing we have that He needs. There is no bribe large enough to bend the will of the Almighty. All power, dominion, and authority already belong to Him—there is nothing we can offer Him that He does not already possess. His will cannot be bent—we know, because Satan tried! In Matthew 4, Jesus was at one of His physically weakest points on earth. He went away into the wilderness to fast and talk to His Father for forty days. In the midst of that weakness, Satan came to Him and offered Him the very best thing that he had to offer: his rule over the world. With one sentence from the Law, Jesus obliterates Satan's scheme:

> *"Get out of here, Satan," Jesus told him. "For the Scriptures say, 'You must worship the LORD your God and serve only him.'" (Matthew 4:10 NLT)*

Apparently, Satan had forgotten that his title as Ruler of this World[11] was only a temporary post—the world

---

11. John 12:31

and everything in it has always belonged its Creator. The best the world has to offer holds no weight for the infinite. When offered the choice between selfishness and true love, Jesus is the only person in existence to have always chosen love.

#JudicialPerfection

The desire for a perfect Judge is hard coded within our very souls. Only God Himself fits the criteria. Romans 2 says that God in His justice will judge humankind. He does not show favoritism. Justice will be finally realized.

> *But because you are stubborn and refuse to turn from your sin, you are storing up terrible punishment for yourself. For a day of anger is coming, when God's righteous judgment will be revealed. He will judge everyone according to what they have done. (Romans 2:5–6 NLT)*

Our hearts long for justice. . .but we should also fear it.

A perfect judge condemns all imperfection, all sin. As we saw in the last chapter, there is no one who escapes sin's reach. We are all tainted. No one can measure up to the mark of perfection that God requires, and thus, we all deserve judgment.

The wrath of God is a theme woven through the whole of the canon, inseparable from divine love. The key might lie in answering the question, "Why is God angry?" As the father of a beautiful little girl, if anyone ever deliberately tried to harm her, my great love for her would be the root of my wrath. How could a truly loving father not react when someone hurts his child? In the same way, God loves us, His creation, so deeply that when sin began to destroy humanity, His love could not stand idly by. The Gospel is rooted in that love. Perfect love and righteous wrath are inseparable when the cancer of sin threatens to contaminate and enslave the people He loves so much.

We can't have justice alone, or we are all doomed. To escape the punishment that is rightfully ours, we need mercy and grace as well. However, there is no way for perfection to simply overlook imperfection. It would be unjust. It would change the nature of perfection itself. God cannot freely give mercy unless He treats us unfairly. We all stand condemned before a perfect, just Judge. The gavel has been struck. The evidence is overwhelming. The situation seems hopeless.

Chapter 3
#RescuePlan

Hope is being able to see that there is light despite all of the darkness.

—DESMOND TUTU

He was used to the darkness. It had long since stopped bothering him. The soft glow of the small light hanging from his neck provided enough illumination for him to dimly see his surroundings. He slouched lower in the passenger seat as the worn-out old truck lumbered down the ramp into the abyss. It wasn't the darkness that bothered him so much as the state of the old mine itself. Just a few years ago, government inspectors had shut down the operation after a fatal accident had claimed the life of a geologist's assistant. In the ensuing fallout, the owners of the San José mine had earnestly promised the government that they would correct the many safety issues that plagued the operation. However, many issues remained unresolved after the dangerous mine was allowed to reopen.

All of that was in the past now, and Jorge Galleguillos

studied the rough-hewn walls in the murky light as they slowly rode past. He was fifty-six, one of the oldest men still working in the dangerous trade. The driver, Franklin Lobos, craned his neck to peer through the gloom, the headlights of the old truck no longer operational. He had only the fog lamps to light his pathway ahead. Deeper into the blackness, and farther from the light of the surface they drove, silently making their way down the four-mile ramp into the belly of the beast. Suddenly, a white streak darted past the truck's windshield.

"Did you see that?" Galleguillos inquired. "That was a butterfly."

"No, it wasn't," Lobos answered. "It was a white rock."

A deafening roar filled the cavern behind them, and walls that had been solid and unyielding seconds ago were now heaving and cracking as the mountain shook around them. The two men instantaneously understood that the mine was collapsing, their greatest fear becoming reality. As Franklin pushed through the cloud of thick dust, the fog lamps of the old vehicle barely penetrated the murky black. A lone figure appeared through the haze, and he slammed the brakes. One by one, the outlines of several other miners and a Toyota pickup materialized. One of them was the shift manager, Florencio Avalos. Several of the men crawled onto the ramshackle personnel truck as Avalos motioned for them to follow his Toyota up the ramp until the path ahead was so littered with fallen rock that they had to get out and walk. Soon the tunnel came to an abrupt halt, as a formidable wall of granite-like rock rose out of the floor in front of them, completely sealing off any exit from the disaster. A single rock weighing several hundred thousand tons had sheared off and fallen to lodge itself into the only way out of the mine.

Within the hour, the men had gathered in a secure break room, deep in the heart of the mine. All connections to the surface had been severed by the disaster—electricity, ventilation, and water. As the full realization of their plight settled in, they took inventory of the supplies they had.

1 can of salmon

1 can of peaches

1 can of peas

18 cans of tuna

24 liters of milk (8 of which turned out to be spoiled)

372 Cartoons (small chocolate- and lemon-flavored sandwich cookies)

10 liters of bottled water

Thousands of liters of water tainted with oil used to cool industrial machinery were also available.

Their eyes locked in the darkness, each of them silently acknowledging the same terrible fact. This was the culmination of all their worst fears. Thirty-three dust-covered figures huddled together in the suffocating blackness, contemplating their fate, wondering if they would ever see the light of day again. Now there was absolutely nothing they could do but wait.[12, 13] They were powerless. Helpless. Doomed.

And so are we.

Paul restates our dire case in Romans 3:10:

As the Scriptures say, "No one is righteous—not even one." (NLT)

The perfect Judge stands in judgment over His creation. All are condemned. The only just and fair action is eternal separation from the Creator. The situation is dire, but God, in His infinite love and kindness, has a plan.

It all started in a garden—not a garden so much as we would think of one, a small plot of soil, dug up with a Rototiller in the springtime with neat rows of peas, carrots, tomatoes, and broccoli all in full bloom. Not a classic English garden either, with tall green hedges, sprawling ivy, and a quiet spot for tea and a book. This garden was a hub of new life, teeming with flora and fauna of amazing diversity, all basking in the wonderment of newborn existence and unencumbered by the trouble and toil that afflict us today. Among the

---

12. Héctor Tobar, "Sixty-nine Days: The Ordeal of the Chilean Miners," *The New Yorker*, July 7, 2014, http://www.newyorker.com/magazine/2014/07/07/sixty-nine-days.

13. *Wikipedia*, s.v. "2010 Copiapó Mining Accident," last modified July 13, 2017, http://en.wikipedia.org/wiki/2010_Copiap%C3%B3_mining_accident.

host of strange and wonderful creatures, there were two extraordinary ones, set apart and unlike any of the others, made in the image of their Maker. To these, the Creator gave special attention. He walked and talked with them. They were more than just His creations; they were His friends. Unlimited food, safety, and health were theirs in abundance—but of all the gifts that their Creator gave them, His presence was by far the greatest. We struggle to understand this concept, but let's stop and consider it. God is the source of every good thing. Every pleasure we enjoy here on earth is merely a pale reflection of Him, untainted by sin, death, or decay. In Him, every need is met, every longing fulfilled. Humankind and God were together in the garden, and God called it good. He also gave them one rule: you may take your pick and eat the fruit of any tree in the garden, but do not eat of the Tree of the Knowledge of Good and Evil. At face value, this seemed simple, but. . . The two people, named Adam and Eve, both disobeyed and ate, and sin entered the world like a 700,000 ton chunk of granite, trapping them both in a tomb of inescapable and eternal death. Through one man, Adam, sin entered the world, and with sin came death, and its effect would ravage the earth. Sin had infected man and separated him from the source of all good—his Creator. Separation from God on earth and the eternal separation that came after death was the worst outcome imaginable. For the first time ever, humankind was presented with the choice of true love or selfishness. We chose wrong. Nothing we could do could remedy the condemnation we had brought upon ourselves. Nothing could wipe away the stain. Nothing could remove the weight. We were all powerless, helpless, and doomed for all eternity, but God was already working out His plan.

In Genesis 3:14–15, the perfect Judge outlines the consequences of sin to the despondent couple, but hidden in this penalty verdict is this glimmer of hope, a tiny glimpse of His rescue plan:

> *Then the* Lord *God said to the serpent, "Because you have done this, you are cursed more than all animals, domestic and wild. You will crawl on your belly, groveling in the dust as long as you live. And I will cause hostility between you and the woman, and between your offspring and her offspring. He will strike your head, and you will strike his heel." (*nlt*)*

Did you catch it? *"He will strike your head, and you will strike his heel."* This passage is known as the *protoevangelium*, or "first Gospel." It is unlikely that Adam and Eve understood the immense significance of this statement. Embedded in this verse is the first foretelling of Jesus—the promise of a future Savior! The snake that tempted Eve was no garden-variety tree serpent. The enemy of heaven, Satan, was present in the garden that day, working to destroy God's creation. God isn't condemning snakes here—He is rebuking the Devil himself. He (Christ) will strike your head, and you (Satan) will strike His heel. Which of those do you think is the fatal blow? The answer would make itself clear thousands of years later on a hill called Golgotha.

There is something else very significant embedded in the text. This glimpse of God's rescue plan was recorded many hundreds of years before it happened. In fact, as we trace the thread of God's grace through history, we see this happen repeatedly. Over and over again, we see promises from God for the future, written down and fulfilled as only He could. These prophecies of our coming Savior stand as beacons of hope in a sea of darkness. The importance of this cannot be understated, not just for a world in darkness waiting for the Light but for you and me today.

Why should we believe that the Bible is true and, more importantly, the Word of the infinite Creator? One powerful proof is fulfilled prophecy. Over the next chapters, we will see some of these incredible prophecies realized. Ancient manuscripts like the Dead Sea Scrolls with specific prophecy about the life and death of Christ far predate the crucifixion. There are hundreds of fulfilled promises in the Bible. Mathematically, the odds of any one of them coming true is tiny, but together the evidence for the divine is staggering. Many have said that faith is blind, but true faith is based on sound reason and fact.

#JustJump

Few leaps in life seem farther and more dangerous than the terrifying divide that spans the distance between a two-year-old and her father standing in waist-deep pool water.

"Jump to me."

In the mind of a toddler, this is the emotional equivalent of leaping out of a plane. Her smiling dad, waiting with arms outstretched, assures her that everything will be fine—that he's right there to catch her. She knows him. She trusts her father—but still, she hesitates. Fear of the unknown has taken hold, and like many who have come before her, it will wreak havoc on her young mind. Her dad, patiently waiting, encourages her, and with one last reassuring glance, she musters up her courage and wholeheartedly launches herself into his arms. What a breathtaking picture of the simple faith that as adults, we so often overcomplicate. Hebrews 11 tells us that faith is the confidence that what we hope will actually happen; it gives us assurance about the things we cannot see. This two-year-old little girl had no prior experience to assure her of the result of leaping into her father's arms. What she did have was the knowledge of what it feels like to have your head slip under the water, and she knew she didn't like that! So what gave her the confidence to risk the jump? Was it blind faith? I would suggest that more than blind faith, it was the fact that she knew and loved the arms that she was leaping toward. She would almost certainly not make that leap into the arms of a stranger. She trusted the relationship with her dad, and her belief that he would catch her outweighed her fear of the water.

Four times in four separate books of the Bible, we are given the directive, "The righteous will live by faith."

"Behold, his soul is puffed up; it is not upright within him, but the righteous shall live by his faith." (Habakkuk 2:4 ESV)

For in it the righteousness of God is revealed from faith for faith, as it is written, "The righteous shall live by faith." (Romans 1:17 ESV)

Now it is evident that no one is justified before God by the law, for "The righteous shall live by faith." (Galatians 3:11 ESV)

"But my righteous one shall live by faith, and if he shrinks back, my soul has no pleasure in him." (Hebrews 10:38 ESV)

One idea, four times, in four separate books is significant. The idea of living by faith is one of the primary threads running throughout the whole of Scripture. From the garden to the end of time, God reinforces the importance of living by faith in His Word. It is one of the central concepts of the Gospel. We have seen already that there is no way for us to remedy our own situation. Where does that leave us? Should we work blindly to impress a perfect God with tainted offerings? Should we throw all we have into the hope that He might defy His own holy and spotless nature, somehow overlook our faults, and accept our fouled gifts? No. He wants us to trust Him and His plan, using reason and the evidence that He has provided us, even when that plan isn't entirely clear yet. No one understood what it meant to live by faith more clearly than our next subject of conversation in God's rescue plan: Abraham.

It was by faith that Abraham obeyed when God called him to leave home and go to another land that God would give him as his inheritance. He went without knowing where he was going. And even when he reached the land God promised him, he lived there by faith—for he was like a foreigner, living in tents. And so did Isaac and Jacob, who inherited the same promise. Abraham was confidently looking forward to a city with eternal foundations, a city designed and built by God. (Hebrews 11:8–10 NLT)

Abraham stood on the edge, looking out over the pool of the unknown, with God calling to him, "Jump!" Doubt and fear swirled in his mind. He was comfortable where he was. Why did God want him to move? Why now? Patiently God reassured him with promises: "I will make you a great nation, a great blessing, and give you a great name."[14] Abram (who hadn't yet had his name changed to Abraham) gathered up his courage and leapt into the life of faith that God had called him to.

The world at that time was a mess. It hadn't been all that long ago that things had gotten so bad that God almost had to hit CTRL-ALT-DELETE and reset the whole production with a worldwide flood. Humankind was a disaster. Selfishness was driving them mad with hatred, greed, and lust. The whole earth was filled with violence.[15] Even in their rebellion, God in His goodness and ever-persistent pursuit of His creation offered a rescue plan. Devastatingly, in this case, no one but Noah and his children accepted it. After a flood washed away the stain of depravity, it quickly began to seep in again. God's next step was to find a man from whom to bring forth a nation that would be a light in this darkness, a

14. Genesis 12:12
15. Genesis 6:13

beacon to point the way back to Him. He found this man in Abram. We should take heart in the fact that Abram had some deeply profound character flaws. God doesn't require perfection in those He uses—merely faith and obedience. That is spectacular news in itself! God called Abram, and Abram obeyed. God made a binding covenant with Abram and changed his name to Abraham and his wife's name to Sarah. He promised the birth of a boy, a promise that Sarah couldn't help but chuckle at given her advanced age. Abraham left for the land God called him to but on the way stopped briefly in Egypt, where an amorous pharaoh had eyes for his wife, Sarah. Instead of trusting God to protect him, he lied and told the pharaoh that she was his sister, hoping the pharaoh wouldn't kill him for his mate. Even still, God patiently rescued Abram from his wicked choices and continued to use him. God did the same thing when a similar situation happened again, some twenty years later. Sarah still did not have her promised son and had given up hope that God would fulfill His promise to her. In desperation, she offered Abram her servant Hagar in hopes that they could conceive a child together. Abram chose wrong—a choice that would prove to be one of the costliest mistakes in all of history. One day, as a ninety-year-old woman, Sarah would conceive the son that God had promised her. The fighting and bloodshed between Hagar's little boy, the modern Arabic nations, and Sarai's son, the Jewish race, still rages unabated today. Even with all this behind him, Abraham's biggest test was yet to come.

There are no words to describe the immense grief left in the wake of the death of a child. It is blinding pain, the kind of suffering that stays with you all hours of the day with no relief. Parents aren't meant to bury their children, and to do so is often considered the most intense grief a person could ever face. *What is happening? What is God thinking? Is this just a bad dream? Why can't I just wake up?* Thoughts like these must have churned over and over in Abraham's head as he took each agonizing step up the side of one of the mountains in the land of Moriah. He had plenty of time to think on the trip from his home to their destination on the mountaintop, with his only son, the ultimate answer to decades of desperate prayers, the sweet fulfillment of a long-awaited promise walking beside him. Isaac was blithely unaware of the impending doom that awaited him at the end of the journey. *God, why? Why Isaac? I just don't understand.* This Abraham was a much different man than the fearful trickster we saw earlier, guarding the things he loved most through any means necessary. The years had taken their toll, and the lines of experience that ran across the old man's weary face were born of wisdom and faith in a

God whom he had learned to trust with his whole heart. Three days earlier, God had spoken to him—not with promises and assurances of wealth and success, but with a request that would shake any father to his very core:

> *"Take your son, your only son—yes, Isaac, whom you love so much—and go to the land of Moriah. Go and sacrifice him as a burnt offering on one of the mountains, which I will show you." (Genesis 22:2 NLT)*

I can imagine what I would have thought. *Child sacrifice! Are you kidding me?* However, full of trembling faith, Abraham trusted God. The very next morning he rose early, packed up, split the wood for the offering, and left for the mountain with Isaac and the modern-day equivalent of two farmhands. The picture of Abraham splitting the wood himself grips me. I can't imagine the raw, nauseating ache of chopping the kindling on which you would later burn the body of the son you just killed.

God will provide a way out.

Maybe that was it. At some point in the trip that thought must have occurred to him. We can be certain of it, because in Genesis 22:5 Abraham says something astounding:

> *"Stay here with the donkey," Abraham told the servants. "The boy and I will travel a little farther.*

We will worship there, and then we will come right back." (NLT)

We will come right back. *We*, not *I*. Even though he couldn't see it, by faith Abraham believed that God would provide a way out, a rescue plan. *I may not see it now. Things may look bleak, but I know and trust the God I serve, and He will make a way.* Abraham looked deep into his Father's eyes, mustered up his courage, and jumped. What an awe-inspiring leap of faith, and for Abraham, it did not go unrewarded. God *did* provide a way out. He never intended for Abraham to kill his own son. That was a task far too heartrending, too excruciating for anyone to be asked to bear. No one should be asked to give up his or her only son as a sacrifice, but God had a rescue plan, and He would stop at nothing to see it through. No pain was too great. No price was too high. No sacrifice was too much to rescue the race of earth dwellers He so deeply loved, so he continued with His plan. He provided a substitute. Sacrificial true love won out over self-preservation. Isaac lived. Abraham became a great nation, the nation of Israel. The rescue plan moved forward, and the flame of hope continued to burn brightly in the darkness.

#

Trapped in the darkness, the thirty-three miners waited for some sign of rescue. There was no way out. Every ventilation shaft, every possible exit strategy had been exhaustively examined. Their limited supplies were growing dangerously thin. One small sandwich cookie every two days was all that their meager stash could allow. In the end, all thirty-three would be liberated from their subterranean tomb and safely returned to their families. What kept them going? How did they survive? I'll give you a clue: it wasn't magical sandwich cookies that kept the miners alive underground for sixty-nine days. It was the hope of an incoming rescue.

Chapter 4

#OfftheMark

Have no fear of perfection—you'll never reach it.
—SALVADOR DALI

The icy wind howled as the figure staggered through the snow. His left leg dragged awkwardly behind him, and the searing pain clouded his mind. The deadly combination of frostbite and gangrene had ravaged it so badly that the night before he had made the costly decision to slash the side of his reindeer-skin sleeping bag to let his leg freeze in a desperate attempt to deaden the pain that tortured him mercilessly. "We came to fight, not to surrender." Those words from the past rang in his ears and haunted him as he stumbled across the frozen landscape. He would never return. He would die in the hope his team could live.

The unforgiving, harsh, stark white of the snow-covered peaks on the pale blue horizon was all they had seen for days. The blinding glare of the sun mercilessly radiated off the snow, burning the eyes of the weary explorers. Their numbers had dwindled to just three—a pitifully small remnant of the original sixteen men who had set out five months earlier. It had taken them years to build their team and carefully plan and prepare, and now all their lofty dreams seemed to be crumbling around them like the white powder that crunched beneath each painful boot step. In a race to discover the South Pole and claim the great fame and fortune that came with it, British explorers Robert Scott, Edward Wilson, and Henry Bowers had lost, and now they were in a desperate race for their survival. The cold whipped about them with relentless fury. With temperatures that at times could drop well below -100°F, their clothes and packs were covered in a formidable layer of heavy ice. Evans had died first, a victim of malnutrition, scurvy, and a head injury, all compounded by the unwavering cold. Just days before, they'd lost Lawrence Oates to their frigid nightmare. His leg had become so consumed with frostbite and gangrene that walking had become all but impossible. Though he had begged his friends to leave him behind so they could make it to the next supply depot before running out of food and crucial fuel for heat, they had refused. They would have never agreed to leave him behind to face certain death alone. Desperate, he had walked out into the blizzard alone in the middle of the night, never to return. His sacrifice still stung in their minds. One of the men stopped to scan the horizon behind them for signs of trouble, and what he saw threatened to drain the last ounces of hope and strength from his fading frame. Another blizzard was fast approaching, ominously racing over the snow in a deadly wall of gray, consuming everything in its path. Their situation was dire. With a dwindling supply of food and fuel, they would need to camp where they were and try and wait the storm out.

The thin canvas walls of the tent did little to ward off the numbing cold from the blizzard that raged outside. Scott lay between his two dead companions, scribbling his last words into a well-worn journal in hopes that someone would one day find their icy final resting place before it was swallowed up in the sea of snow and ice.

We very nearly came through, and it's a pity to have missed it, but lately I have felt that we have overshot our mark. [16]

Every day we have been ready to start for our depot 11 miles away, but outside the door of the tent it remains a scene of whirling drift. I do not think we can hope for any better things now. We shall stick it out to the end, but we are getting weaker, of course, and the end cannot be far. It seems a pity but I do not think I can write more. R. Scott. Last entry. For

16. Karen May, "Could Captain Scott have been saved? Revisiting Scott's last expedition," *Polar Record* 49, no. 1 (2013): 72–90, doi:10.1017/S0032247411000751. Accessed 6 July 2014.

God's sake look after our people.[17]

We have overshot our mark. Those words hardly do justice to contain the absolute hopelessness and despair Scott must have felt in that moment as he lay dying in the Antarctic. There would be no survivors. *Where did I go wrong? What did I miss? How did it come to this?*

#PromiseKept

Abraham was dead, but the promise lived on, first through his son Isaac, and then his grandson Jacob. Working not just in spite of but *through* their flaws, God faithfully guided His rescue plan along. Abraham's seed would become a great nation, but not before a series of unfortunate events led Jacob's clan down to Egypt. Joseph, one of Jacob's sons, both summarized the current situation and foreshadowed God's eventual rescue plan without realizing it:

> *You intended to harm me, but God intended it all for good. He brought me to this position so I could save the lives of many people. (Genesis 50:20 NLT)*

It was there in Egypt, over time, that the "nation" began to take shape. The offspring of Jacob, or "Israel" multiplied so quickly that the pharaoh took notice and

---

17. Leonard Huxley, *Scott's Last Expedition,* vol. 1 (*London: Smith, Elder & Co, 1913)*, 583–95.

began to feel threatened by the mass of outsiders on his lands. He decided that the best course of action was to enslave the Israelites and treat them with unspeakable cruelty. Incredibly, the tougher things became for Jacob's people, the more they multiplied—infuriating the Egyptian leadership. Things got progressively worse. Slave labor, harsh treatment, even the systematic slaughter of their children by the Egyptians took their toll, and soon, Abraham's descendants were wondering if God had completely forgotten them. *How did things get this bad? Where did we go wrong?*

God had not forgotten. The rescue plan had not been thwarted, and God was about to raise up a leader for an expedition the likes of which the world had never seen. First, He had to forge a leader to fit the task ahead.

Fearing the Israelites, Pharaoh had decreed that every baby boy born to a Hebrew family was to be murdered at birth. Under this threat, Moses was born. To keep him safe, he was hidden in the undergrowth near the Nile River each day in hopes that soldiers would not discover and kill him as they searched the Israelite homes for male babies to murder. Moses' sister was to watch over him, and one can only imagine the terror she must have felt as he lay in that reed basket one day crying loudly as a group of Egyptians came down to the river. He was discovered, but by a princess, not a soldier, and her heart melted at the sight of the helpless little baby. God miraculously worked things out so that Moses would be raised by his own mother then trained in the palace of Egypt in virtually the best schools in the entire world. After he had become a young man, Moses went out and started to observe the harsh conditions his fellow Israelites were groaning under and happened upon one of the Egyptian taskmasters brutally beating a Hebrew. His temper flared, and Moses murdered the slaver in cold blood. Clearly, this didn't sit well with his adoptive mom's dad, the pharaoh, and Moses was forced to run for his life, out of Egypt, all the way to a backwater, sheepherding, wilderness land called Midian. *What had just happened? Where did he go wrong? How did things get this bad?*

To the naked eye, it looked like Moses' life had been ruined, but God was still at work. The lessons he would learn over the next forty years in the Midianite desert—herding sheep, learning to live off the land, and keeping his flock from killing themselves—would prove essential in the work God had planned for him. Moses' life is a reminder that even when we feel like we have broken things beyond repair, God is still working. The Bible reminds us that the righteous will live by faith, not by flawless decision-making and mistake-free choices. God allowed Moses to spend time in the desert before tasking him with the unthinkable. God was about to stage the greatest jailbreak the world had ever seen. Hundreds of thousands of men, women, and children were about to escape from the best-trained and best-equipped standing army of the day, and that was just the beginning.

#Recalibration

Fire. In the right place, it can be useful, warm, and inviting and bring light to a dark place. In the wrong place, it can usher in disaster. On this day, it was neither. In all of his years of wandering the wilderness, sheep at his side, Moses had never seen anything like the strange spectacle in front of him. Flames licked at the branches of the dry desert shrub, but somehow the shrub wasn't burning up. I love how Scripture records this moment in Exodus 3:3:

"This is amazing," Moses said to himself. "Why isn't that bush burning up? I must go see it."

I wonder if Moses said those words aloud. Had he been out with the sheep for so long that he had begun to talk to himself? Whatever the reason, the display of the fiery bush must have been a sight to behold. When God wants to capture our attention, He doesn't mess around. God identified Himself to Moses as the God of Abraham, Isaac, and Jacob for a reason. He had not forgotten His promise, nor had He abandoned His people. His rescue plan was still in motion. God set out His plan to pull

Moses' people from the jaws of their captors and set them on a great expedition to a land He had chosen for them, and Moses panics. Maybe he remembered how afraid he was the day he ran from Egypt. Perhaps he felt that his checkered past made him an unfit leader—someone far too damaged for God to use. Maybe, like so many of us, Moses was simply fearful of a future that held more question marks than he was comfortable with. It was at this moment that God, for the first time recorded in the Bible, introduced Himself by the name I AM.

I AM.

Constraints of the English language prevent us from fully grasping the significance of these three letters. The Infinite is introducing Himself to the finite. I AM. The great mystery of the divine is unfolding before human eyes. Just like a single coffee cup cannot hold the entire Pacific Ocean, we stagger under the weight and magnitude of the sheer glory, power, and wisdom of the Almighty. We cannot hope to fully understand His entirety, *but* He has revealed aspects of Himself to us. This is one of those aspects. I AM.

This is my eternal name, my name to remember for all generations. (Exodus 3:15 NLT)

God is opening the eyes of Moses to who He is. God is timeless. Take a moment to deeply consider that. We are temporal beings, in a world where one of the dimensions we are bound by is time. We have no ability to process a being outside of this construct. I AM. Just as God is not bound by height, depth, or width, He cannot be contained by time. Moses desperately needed this recalibration of his perspective on who God is. In that moment, the threat of Pharaoh's wrath, Moses' own past failures, and his perceived inadequacies were all bigger in his mind than the infinite power of the God before whom he knelt, shoeless in the desert. If God was going to be able to use Moses in His rescue plan, he was going to need an infusion of reality, STAT. The old rules were no more. His eyes were being opened to something much bigger and far more amazing than he could have ever dreamed. Moses needed to recalibrate his mind to a new reality. In Exodus 4, we see God about to do just that.

The Infinite has just revealed Himself personally to Moses and laid out His plan to rescue the line of Abraham. It was impossible for Moses' mind to wrap itself around the magnitude and power of the God he was kneeling before. Over the next few verses in Exodus, God worked with His servant, a wise master opening the eyes of his student to true reality. The God that created the planets and stars had the patience to do something as simple as turn a stick into a snake so His budding expedition leader might begin to grasp the incredible power his Master wields. A small step forward. Watch me turn your hand white with leprosy and heal it again. Another step. I can also turn rivers to blood. Yet another step. There is so much significance here. This first recorded personal interaction between Moses and God is so much bigger than it might seem at first glance. The Creator is making Himself known to His creation, but there is so much baggage in the way. Moses is blinded by his past failure, his current insecurities, and the fear of the future unknown. He has trouble grasping the concept that the One who controls all things is recruiting him for a role in a grand plan of redemption that stretches far beyond the Hebrew slaves held captive in Egypt. I AM is speaking directly and personally to him. God describes the terrible plagues he will send on Egypt to loosen the crippling grasp of Pharaoh on the children of Abraham. Slowly, Moses' eyes begin to open—but still, the excuses continue. He complains about his ability to speak eloquently to the Grand Designer of his tongue. In hindsight, that might not have been the wisest move, because in verse 14 God begins to grow angry. He allows Moses to bring his brother Aaron along as a stand-in speaker, but Moses is still God's choice to lead the expedition. What a reassuring reminder that God uses flawed people. Moses' perspective realignment is complete, for now, and he chooses to obey.

#SetFree

The Nile runs thick and red with blood. Frogs cover the land like a pulsing blanket of croaking green invaders. Disease, dangerous hailstorms, swarms of flies and locusts, and a suffocating darkness are all inflicted upon the Egyptians as God readies His people for a mass exodus out of Egypt. Each plague seems to harden Pharaoh's heart even more, and he refuses to allow the Israelites to leave. But God has one final, devastating plague to send. Moses calls the Hebrews together and explains that God plans to kill the firstborn child of every family in Egypt. To save their children, Moses instructs each Israelite household to select a lamb with no defect and separate it from the rest of the flock. The Hebrews were primarily sheepherders, so this would have been a simple task. Moses shared that the people were to take special care of this lamb for three days, and then on the fourteenth day of the month, they were to kill the lamb, cook and eat it, and use its blood to mark their doorways.

> *For the LORD will pass through the land to strike down the Egyptians. But when he sees the blood on the top and sides of the doorframe, the LORD will pass over your home. He will not permit his death angel to enter your house and strike you down. (Exodus 12:23 NLT)*

> *Death will see the blood and pass over.* For centuries,

the people of Israel would continue to mark this day on their calendars, just as God had instructed. For centuries, blood would be spilled from a lamb, chosen without flaw or blemish to be sacrificed that others could live. For centuries, the people of God would celebrate the night that God rescued them from bondage—a night that would come to be called Passover.

#RockandaHardPlace

Chaos. Confusion. Panic. *Did we come all this way just to die?* With one of the best-trained and most technologically advanced armies in the world bearing down on them like a pack of ravenous wolves, the Hebrews were sitting ducks. The lumbering mass of newly liberated travelers was no match for the speed of the elite chariots of the fearsome Egyptian fighting force. They had nowhere to go and everything to lose. Pinned in on one side by the Red Sea and on the other by a host of deadly warriors that were closing in fast, the Hebrews were beginning to lose faith in their new expedition leader. Just days earlier, God had miraculously broken the shackles of their bondage to Egypt with incredible displays of power that had left all of the Nile River Valley reeling. They had been in such a hurry to help the Israelites pack that many had donated valuable items and goods of their own as they left, and now the people of the Nile wanted it all back, along with their slave labor. At that moment, some of the people started to vocalize their dissent:

> *"Why did you bring us out here to die in the wilderness? Weren't there enough graves for us in Egypt? What have you done to us? Why did you make us leave Egypt? Didn't we tell you this would happen while we were still in Egypt? We said, 'Leave us alone! Let us be slaves to the Egyptians. It's better to be a slave in Egypt than a corpse in the wilderness!'"* (Exodus 14:11–12 NLT)

If Moses had been using a GPS, I'm sure at that moment it would have cheerfully announced, "Recalculating." Moses had every reason to panic. It is one thing to be in grave danger, but when you are responsible for the lives of thousands of others, the stress level skyrockets. *How did things get this bad? Where did we go wrong?*

Several years ago, I spent some time in the police station of a small town in Costa Rica with a group of high school girls and a coleader of a mission trip as we waited to be processed. There is nothing like standing in a police station in a foreign country and being responsible for the welfare of a group of others. Earlier that day, our group of students and leaders had spent the afternoon with a small local church in the mountainous regions of Costa Rica, assisting them in a weeklong summer event that they were hosting for children in their village. We played games, sang songs, and had a blast with the little ones as they drank in the creative atmosphere and the love that the church members poured out on the children of their community. As the day drew to a close, we walked the few miles of dirt roads back to the compound we were housed at, only to find that the building the girls were staying in had been vandalized. Much of the luggage had been rummaged through, and any items of value had been stolen. The robbery had also stolen any sense of security the group had. Here we were, thousands of miles from the familiar, and suddenly we found ourselves faced with something that threatened to derail our mission.

Moses' mission was in jeopardy as well. Pinned down with nowhere to run, the people were beginning to turn on him. Beautifully, this is where we see the time spent with God at the burning bush finally begin to sink in. God had opened Moses' eyes to His power, and Moses was beginning to understand true reality.

> But Moses told the people, "Don't be afraid. Just stand still and watch the LORD rescue you today. The Egyptians you see today will never be seen again. The LORD himself will fight for you. Just stay calm." (Exodus 14:13–14 NLT)

Recalibration successful. Through the blizzard of pressure and strife, in the face of seemingly overwhelming odds, having buried the past failures that had haunted him for so long, Moses can see the reality of God's power and the inevitability of His unstoppable rescue plan more clearly than ever. If faith is the assurance of the unseen, Moses was walking by faith in a way he had never done before, and God was about to use His servant in breathtaking ways.

Back in Costa Rica, we had finished filing our report with the local authorities. Thankfully my coleader was fluent in Spanish, because my competency level is on par with about two or three seasons of *Dora the Explorer*. Later that night at our group study time, we talked about the day's events. It was amazing to see the kids open up about how they were feeling and to watch God begin to use a seemingly terrible incident to recalibrate their perspectives about why they were even there. Sometimes the things that matter are not the ones that seem the most significant at first glance.

#MissedtheMark

Robert Scott lay dying in his tent, the icy wind howling outside, a macabre soundtrack to the final scene in his tragic journey. The frozen corpses of two of his companions lay beside him, and he knew it was only a matter of hours before the cold would claim his life as well.

Antarctica was a harsh teacher, and soon the blizzard would swallow their little tent in a sea of white. He wondered if anyone would ever read the words he penned in his last hours.

We very nearly came through, and it's a pity to have missed it, but lately I have felt that we have overshot our mark. No-one is to blame and I hope no attempt will be made to suggest that we had lacked support.[18]

The race to the South Pole had been lost. The group had failed miserably, and somehow, even in the face of this catastrophic failure, Robert Scott pens the words, "No-one is to blame." This is one of the most frightening things about Scott's leadership of the Terra Nova Expedition. Even to the very end, he was unable to see where he had gone wrong. There were many things that may have ultimately doomed the men on Scott's trip to the disaster it became. He chose to rely heavily on ponies instead of sled dogs for travel, most of which were not in spectacular shape to begin with. He trusted untested technology by using motorized sleds that quickly broke down in the harsh environment of the Antarctic. He geared his men with heavy wool clothing that accumulated layers of ice on the outside and moisture on the inside, instead of

18. Karen May, "Could Captain Scott have been saved? Revisiting Scott's last expedition," *Polar Record* 49, no. 1 (2013): 72–90, doi:10.1017/S0032247411000751.

the furs that native peoples of the subfreezing climates wore for their better performance. Scott did not plan well for the health of his team by including provisions with the vitamins needed to ward off scurvy, a crippling condition that had a hand in claiming the life of more than one of his men. These were just some of the issues that caused one of the deadliest exploratory disasters in recent history. Robert Falcon Scott had indeed missed the mark, but most dangerous of all, he did not see his error even in the end.

#MountainofFlame

Moses stood at the foot of the mountain with the descendants of Abraham cowering behind him. It wasn't the first time that Moses had seen something strange burning in the wilderness, but this time, instead of a bush, a mountain of flame rose up before him. Earthquake tremors shook the ground under his feet. The Infinite had come to meet with His people. Three months had passed since the day the Hebrews had walked out of Egypt and started on their expedition into the wilderness and toward the Promised Land. During that time, it had become abundantly clear that this ragtag bunch of wilderness wanderers knew very little about the God who had rescued them from bondage and was guiding them to their new home. It was time for some revelation. On Mount Sinai that day, the Creator gave them much more than they bargained for. The power and majesty on display caused the Hebrews to shrink back in fear, but this was only the beginning. God called Moses up the mountain to talk. The next step in His rescue plan for the world was about to be revealed.

For hundreds of years, God had watched as the people of Earth, His beloved creation, had brutalized themselves and each other. This was not His design. Greed, pride, and lust drive humans to unthinkable depravity. Even now, we don't have to look further than the front page of any major news site or publication to see the treachery and evil humankind has wrought on itself. When God intervened through Moses on Mount Sinai, He set in place guidelines that would curb the grisly torrent of human suffering due to selfishness. He gave His people a code to follow out of love. There are two things here that we must establish before we go on. First, the main motivation for God is His own glory, and second, God has designed the world to work in a certain way.

God is for His glory, but we are for ours.

#MyWay

We live in a culture and world that bombards us on a daily basis with messages of narcissism and self-centeredness.

Billions of dollars are spent each year on advertising campaigns and slogans to feed our narcissism.

"Just do it."—Nike

"Have it your way."—Burger King

"Treat yourself well."—Dasani (Coca-Cola)

"Love the way you look."—Men's Warehouse

From advertising to art, movies to social media, the idea of self-importance and admiration is everywhere. This should come as no surprise. After all, it was that same marketing campaign that greased the wheels for sin to edge its way into the world from the start. "You will be like God." If that doesn't play to our human egotism, I don't know what does. It can be very easy then to look at the Gospel from a very human-centric point of view, where the chief goal of God's rescue plan is to save humankind. It is so much more. Time and time again, the same phrase is repeated throughout Scripture: *for the glory of God*. In the first few sentences of Paul's letter to the Romans, Paul cuts to the heart of the motivation for sharing the Gospel with the world:

> *This letter is from Paul, a slave of Christ Jesus, chosen by God to be an apostle and sent out to preach his Good News. God promised this Good News long ago through his prophets in the holy Scriptures. The Good News is about his Son. In his earthly life he was born into King David's family line, and he was*

shown to be the Son of God when he was raised from the dead by the power of the Holy Spirit. He is Jesus Christ our Lord. Through Christ, God has given us the privilege and authority as apostles to tell Gentiles everywhere what God has done for them, so that they will believe and obey him, bringing glory to His name. Romans 1:1–5 (NLT, emphasis added)

There it is. God's chief aim in the rescue of humankind is bringing glory to His name. Does the idea of God being primarily concerned with His name and glory seem egocentric? C. S. Lewis, one of the great Christian thinkers of the last century, struggled with the same questions before his conversion while teaching medieval literature at Oxford University. To him, God seemed no better than an old lady fishing for compliments. "Praise me. Worship me. How does my hair look? Does this dress make me look fat? Everything is for my glory." I have to confess, I've had similar questions. Not about my hairstyle or wardrobe, mind you, but why God seems to want our worship and praise so badly. It isn't as though He needs us for anything. The Uncreated One existed for eternity and got along splendidly without us, so why all the focus on His glory now? Lewis writes about this subject in the essay, "The Problem of Praise in the Psalms."

It is in the process of being worshipped that God communicates His presence to men. It is not, of course, the only way. But for many people at many times the "fair beauty of the Lord" is revealed chiefly or only while they worship Him together. Even in Judaism the essence of the sacrifice was not really that men gave bulls and goats to God, but that by their so doing God gave Himself to men; in the central act of our own worship of course this is far clearer—there it is manifestly, even physically, God who gives and we who receive. The miserable idea that God should in any sense need, or crave for, our worship like a vain woman wanting compliments, or a vain author presenting his new books to people who never met or heard him, is implicitly answered by the words, "If I be hungry I will not tell thee" (50:12). Even if such an absurd Deity could be conceived, He would hardly come to us, the lowest of rational creatures, to gratify His appetite.[19]

God is for His own glory, and we are all the better for it. In worship it is not humankind that is doing the giving, but God revealing His nature to us in reminders of His goodness and love. We will never experience true joy apart from the source of all joy. We will never find true peace apart from the One who gives peace that passes all understanding. Every good thing originates in Him. God wants us to worship Him for His glory and our joy. There

19. C. S. Lewis, *Reflections on the Psalms* (Great Britain: Fontana Books, 1958).

can be no joy or fulfillment apart from Him—indeed, hell itself is the culmination of telling God to "get out!" It is the complete removal of God's presence with us.

Technology is great when it works. When it doesn't, the resulting fallout can be a disaster. Robert Scott found this out the hard way when he decided to take newly invented motor sledges with him on his failed expedition. These new triumphs of innovation were supposed to have been able to haul heavy amounts of gear and supplies, but they were plagued with issues and finally broke down just fifty miles into the journey.[20] Unbelievably, the designer and inventor of the machines, who no doubt would have been instrumental in their upkeep and repair, was forced off the expedition by a petty leadership dispute, so the main transport strategy failed. Scott had spent almost seven times the amount of money on his motor sledges than on the dogs and horses combined, yet he had failed to plan for their maintenance. He failed to see what seems obvious in retrospect: that the designer knows how best to run and care for his creations.

Before we are too quick to point the finger at Scott, let's remember how often we make the same mistake. God has designed the world to work in a certain way, but all too often, we reject the guidelines and wisdom He has given us because it doesn't seem right for us. Can you see

---

20. Roland Huntford, *The Last Place on Earth* (New York: Random House, 1983), 404.

the absurdity here? When we reject the principles that God has set for us in His Word, we are effectively saying, "Look, God, I know You designed and created everything. You know every aspect of every human who ever lived, is living, or will live. You invented and know the intricate inner workings of our universe in a way that thousands of millennia of scientific discovery will only scratch the surface. You understand the machinations of the heart of the human race and still love them. But on this occasion, I'm pretty sure the experience of my relative cosmic blink of an existence trumps Your eternal infinite wisdom." Sometimes the instruction might not be clear. Sometimes the command given is difficult to follow. Sometimes we misinterpret divine direction because we are too busy to search the Scriptures to verify its authenticity. No matter what the scenario, trusting God and walking in faith will always lead to the best eternal result. When we trust the Designer, His wisdom is never faulty. God is for His own glory, and we are all the better for it.

Flash back to the mountain of fire, where Moses is busy transcribing God's newly minted laws and regulations for His recently freed people. The descendants of Abraham wait nervously at the bottom of the towering inferno. What will God say?

The result is a volume of rules and rituals that take up a large portion of four of the first five books in our modern-day Bible. On that mountain, God laid out the requirements for man to be able to reconnect with Him. A perfect and just God can demand no less than perfection. The standard was set. The mark was made. The requirements were clear. You will worship no other gods. Don't murder people. Don't have sex with someone you aren't married to. Don't steal. Respect your parents. Don't lie. God gave Moses the ground rules for His people, rules that protected them from each other and allowed them to live in community, rules that protected them from themselves. God gave us the Law.

#Identity

Sporting events in the United States can lead to some pretty strange places. Spectators throw eight-legged cephalopods onto the ice during a hockey game. Some football fans wear hats that look like giant wedges of cheese. Others come to outdoor games in freezing temperatures, wearing nothing above the waist but paint. Team colors, mascots, chants, and clothing can add a degree of intimidation to a home stadium, adding an extra few degrees of difficulty for any adversary. Some of us diehard fans can get pretty attached to a team. We use terms like "us" and "our" instead of "they" and "their" when describing the latest exploits or shortfalls of our favorite team. When our team does well, we are elated. When they lose, we are crushed. For some reason, our very identity is tied to a sports team. As God presented Israel with the Law, He also gave them another gift, a way to preserve their identity. Their Creator was calling them to be holy, or set apart from all the other nations on the earth. In the Law, we see two separate means to accomplish this with distinct types of rules. One is ritual law, and the other is ethical law. There is an enormous difference between "Don't murder people" and "Don't eat bacon." A ritual is a habit or ceremony used to set something apart and/or give significance to an act. God wanted His people to remember who and whose they were, giving them rules to follow every day that constantly reminded them to do this. Ethical law set them apart morally from the world around them. It was there to protect them from each other and help them to live peaceably in community. It was there to protect them from themselves. This law reminded them of the standard of perfection of the holy God they worshipped. It exposed their inability to measure up and their inevitable missing of the mark. The law opened their eyes to the solemn truth that despite their recent rescue from the hands of their captors in Egypt, they were still unable to escape the prison of sin forged by their own rebellion. The law ultimately exposes our undeniable need for a Savior.

# #

In the end, there were many reasons that Robert Scott's expedition to the South Pole failed so drastically, only one of which was his choice in navigational logistics. There were two main options Scott had at his disposal for the trip. One was the sextant: a light, fairly straight-forward instrument used to calculate position by the sun, moon, and stars. It was widely used, and most explorers could navigate by it. The second was the theodolite, a heavy, complex, yet precise piece of equipment, and only a single man in Scott's expedition knew how to operate it. Scott chose the latter. The most precise equipment available is of no use if no one is able to use it. On another team in their competition in the race to the South Pole, almost every man knew how to navigate, and it showed. It was part of the difference between triumph and failure. A man will never find his way again if he does not first come to the realization that he has lost it to begin with.

Humanity was thrashing blindly in the darkness, with no regard for the damage it inflicted on itself or the world it called home. The Law broke through like a blazing beacon of light, illuminating the desperation of our state. In its glow, we can see more clearly the carnage our choices have wrought and see the fallout of a path diverged from the design of the Creator. Maybe we blame

God for the consequences of the mess we have made as a collective human race. Maybe, despite His incredible love and mercy, we continue to reject Him, turning to a temporary empty solace of our own design, and when that slips through our fingers like sand through an hourglass, we clench them into a fist to shake at the very One who offers true eternal peace. Maybe we lie back in our own polar expeditionary tents, cursing the blizzard around us, and wait to die, abandoning all hope.

Or maybe we don't.

Maybe there is still a flicker of hope alive, burning softly but brightly.

Chapter 5

#NotAbandoned

The loneliest moment in someone's life is when they are watching their whole world fall apart, and all they can do is stare blankly.

—F. Scott Fitzgerald

Fiery red paint with two black racing stripes cut a path down the center of the small race car. Gleaming chrome rims wrapped with jet black tires and real working headlights drew him in like a moth to the flame. At five years old, this was the most beautiful thing he had ever laid eyes on, and he was captivated. He stood for what seemed like hours, staring, wishing, dreaming of the fun he could have with the toy car on the shelf before him. Suddenly, when the boy looked up, he felt all the joy drain out of him. His throat tightened. His pulse raced. His breathing quickened. He was all alone. He panicked, his eyes frantically scanning the aisle in the spot where just moments ago his father had stood. Tears began to pool in his eyes, and he quickly blinked them away and bit into his quivering lower lip. *This can't be happening.* Maybe he was simply in the next aisle. The red race car that had briefly been the center of his world was a distant memory now. He raced past a display of foam weaponry that would have been a fascinating discovery mere seconds ago, rounded the endcap of spaceship LEGOs, and burst into the next aisle, pink everywhere. A woman looked up from the Malibu Barbie she was examining, but she wasn't the person he was looking for. *Where is he? How could he leave me like this?* He raced from aisle to aisle, barely contained anxiety rising in his chest. He searched and searched, but his father was nowhere to be found. Finally, he gave in to the fear and collapsed in a heap next to a pile of overstuffed assorted farm animals, quietly sobbing. He was utterly alone. Abandoned.

Most of us have had an experience like this in our lifetimes. We've been left behind at a gas station on a family road trip or gotten lost in the mall. We've been forgotten at home during the family's Christmas vacation and forced to defend it from two blundering would-be robbers while our mother frantically tried to find her way home. (Wait, that last one was actually a movie. . .) Some have had even tougher experiences. Many have been abandoned by a parent, betrayed by a friend, or cheated on by an unfaithful spouse.

#Abandoned

This is how the people of Israel must have felt as they were led away in chains from the land God had given them. Their homes and cities were a smoldering ruin. Many of their friends and family members had been slaughtered. Everything they had held dear was either destroyed or pillaged by the most formidable army they had ever seen. They were now slaves to an empire blazing a trail of fury and flame throughout the known world. There would be no rescue now. *Where was God? What had happened to His grand rescue plan?* As the descendants of Abraham stumbled into Babylonian captivity, these are some of the things they must have wondered. But this terrible fate had not come without warning.

After a time in the wilderness with Moses, God had led His people to victory in Canaan. Under the leadership of Joshua, Israel had routed their enemies and conquered the land promised to them by God, but they had not finished the task God had set them on. The Canaanite people who had remained in the land pulled the hearts of the Hebrews away from God, enticing them to worship fake gods and reject the One who had rescued them out of Egypt and led them through the desert. God had sent messengers and prophets to warn His people of the consequences of their evil choices, but they had seldom listened. They had turned their backs on the rescue plan and disobeyed the Law set in place to protect them from themselves, so God removed His protection and allowed other nations to come in and oppress them. In their distress, they cried out to God until He sent a savior to rescue them. Things would go better for a while, but it was only a matter of time until God's chosen people would cycle back into *apostasy,* or rejection of their commitment to God. Over and over the children of Abraham cast aside the God of their fathers, only to be ravaged by the consequences of their sin until it felt unbearable and they begged His forgiveness. This cycle continued for hundreds of years, each time seemingly worse than before, until finally God had enough. Assyria and Babylon swept into a divided nation of Israel like a tsunami, crushing anything and everyone in their path and dragging away what was left, leaving behind nothing but twisted wreckage and shattered dreams. This disaster had not come without warning, but time after time the chosen people ignored the words of God's messengers and dismissed the warnings of His prophets.

#InvisibleArmy

Elisha was one of these prophets,[21] and it was almost dawn when his servant crawled out of bed to begin the day. With much to do, he quickly set about with the morning's business. Lighting a fire, gathering water, and preparing the morning meal were all routine tasks that he was well accustomed to, but when he stepped out into the brisk air, he staggered back in disbelief. From his vantage point, he could see an enormous army of horses, soldiers, and chariots surrounding the city. He knew precisely why they were there, and it was no peacekeeping mission. For some time, his master had been helping the king of Israel. When enemies moved their troops or made plans to attack, God would tell Elisha, and he would relay the message to the king, always staying a step ahead. This infuriated the king of Aram so much that he had finally sent an entire army, with the best military technology available at the time, to kill one man. The day of reckoning had finally come. One can only imagine the fear that gripped the heart of Elisha's servant as he surveyed the host of warriors that had come for the lives of him and his master. They were completely surrounded. *Had God forgotten them? Had he abandoned His servants? How could they ever muster a force strong enough to fend off the attacking horde?* There

---

21. 2 Kings 6:1–17

was no way out, no escape. The servant's knees buckled as he mentally recounted the stories he'd heard of the brutality of marauding armies laying waste to other cities. He rushed back into the house to bang on the door of his master's room. "Elisha, Elisha!" The tranquility he found in his master's eyes was uncanny. As the servant hurriedly explained the dire situation, Elisha sat, unmoved, nodding peacefully, until at last the servant could no longer stand it. "Master, what are we going to do!" he blurted out. His master smiled, and then opened his mouth to pray these simple words: *"Lord, open his eyes that he may see."*

Elisha didn't ask God for a fireball from heaven. He didn't ask to be magically teleported away to safety. He didn't even ask for superpowers. The prophet simply requested perspective for his servant. God answered his prayer and opened the eyes of the servant. Instantly, he could see that the hillside all around them was teeming with an army of their own—but not an ordinary army. It was literally on fire! This was a vast angelic defense force, any one of which could have wiped out the entirety of the king of Aram's army. Their enemy had believed he was coming with an overwhelming force, yet he was more outmatched than a birthday candle in a hurricane. Think of the relief that must have flooded over the servant as he realized how safe he was. God was in control. He had a rescue plan. He had not abandoned them. Now, here is the remarkable thing: nothing actually changed. The heavenly legion was there long before Elisha prayed. God had merely opened the servant's eyes to see. *Merriam-Webster's* dictionary defines *perspective* as "the capacity to view things in their true relations or relative importance."[22] God had not left His servants, just like He had never left His people even through the many cycles of disobedience and consequences.

The Gospel at its core is God's rescue plan to reunite humankind with Himself. He has never walked away. Through times when it seems all is lost, He remains steadfast. His faithfulness is everlasting to the ones who trust in Him, sometimes despite our failure of epic proportion. Not every prophet was a paragon of righteousness. One of my favorite depictions of the Gospel in the Old Testament is in the book of Jonah. If the Gospel is God's redemptive plan to restore the broken relationship between Himself and humanity, in this story we see it in multiple layers. So often the God of the Old Testament is described as one of fire and fury, a judge, jury, and executioner. He is harsh and hard, while the God of the New Testament is portrayed as one of love and mercy, gentle and kind, with forgiveness to all

---

22. Merriam-Webster OnLine, s.v. "perspective," accessed July 19, 2017, http://www.merriam-webster.com/dictionary/perspective.

who ask for it. This could not be further from the truth. I AM who spoke with Moses from the burning bush has been, is, and will always be the same God. His character is unchanging. A great example of this is found in Jonah, where God sends the prophet with a message of redemption for the city of Nineveh. This key Assyrian city was no stranger to savagery. Psychological warfare was a key part of the Assyrian strategy, and they were a particularly brutal enemy with a fearsome reputation well known in Jonah's day. As their army ravaged the land, they left behind horrifying monuments to their ruthlessness: impaled bodies on long poles, heaps of human heads, dismembered and mutilated corpses, and piles of human skins from unsubmissive leaders who had been flayed alive.[23] The very fact that God was concerned about the fate of the people of this city is telling. He always has been, and always will be, a God interested in the redemption of all nations. He did not change in the New Testament—He has always, *always* been in the process of redeeming humanity. So Jonah, instead of obeying and going to preach the message God had given him for the Ninevites, rebelled and ran the other way. Even then, God did not abandon Jonah. He could have rightly punished Jonah for his disobedience, but instead God went out of His way to do something miraculous. He created a place for Jonah to think about

23. http://cojs.org/grisly-assyrian-record-of-torture-and-death/

his life for three days, in the belly of a fish. Don't miss this. God is not just a God of the nameless masses. He cared about Jonah deeply and individually, enough to craft an incredible set of circumstances to bring him to the truth. This is the Gospel. It is the good news of hope and redemption for an undeserving city condemned to destruction. It is the good news of life and forgiveness for a prophet who had been blinded by selfishness and fear. It is the good news of a God who is actively pursuing all nations to be restored to Himself, no matter what the cost.

#FatherlyPerspective

To say the day had been a busy one would have been an understatement. Work had been incredibly busy lately, and his boss had given no sign that things were going to get better anytime soon. With three large projects all converging, the deadlines circled like vultures over their prey. He had almost forgotten to pick up the birthday present his wife had ordered for their youngest daughter from the local toy store. Thankfully she had texted him earlier as he stood watching his five-year-old son run, arms flailing and legs churning, in a swarming mass of other boys around a small round ball, in what could only be called a valiant attempt at youth soccer. Having no time to spare, the father carefully instructed his son to stay close beside him in the toy store. They were in a hurry and needed to be quick about their errand. When they reached the store, he went straight to the service desk, and out of the corner of his eye, he saw his son, enamored by a shiny red race car, drift off into one of the aisles. The line in front of him moved quickly, and soon the toy they had ordered was in his hands. As he walked to the checkout to pay for the gift, he noticed his son look up from the red car he was holding. He could see the boy's eyes searching for him, so he called and waved him over to the checkout line as he pulled out his wallet to pay. The little boy did not see or hear. The father paid for the toy as quickly as he could as he watched his little boy run from aisle to aisle looking for him. As he walked toward him he called out again, but at this point the child was in such a panic, he heard nothing and crumpled in a heap of tears into a pile of overstuffed farm animals.

#GlimmersofHope

Isaiah's life took place during one of the darker times in the history of God's people. He was a prophet who lived during the time when Assyria had begun to invade the land. In the midst of all this, God used his prophet Isaiah to plead with His people to turn from their wickedness and be spared from the coming atrocities. Isaiah writes this in his opening chapter:

"Come now, let's settle this,"
  says the LORD.
"Though your sins are like scarlet,
  I will make them as white as snow.
Though they are red like crimson,
  I will make them as white as wool.
If you will only obey me,
  you will have plenty to eat.
But if you turn away and refuse to listen,
  you will be devoured by the sword of your enemies.
I, the LORD, have spoken!" (Isaiah 1:18–21 NLT)

Sadly, the nation of Israel did not listen, and in the coming years their suffering was immense. All seemed lost. The descendants of Abraham had become scattered and broken. Had God finally abandoned His people?

In the darkness shone a glimmer of light. One of the roles of a prophet in Scripture is to warn of impending disastrous consequences when people chase after sin, but there is another, more hopeful, role as well. In his book, Isaiah pulls back the curtain and reveals more of God's divine rescue plan than has ever been seen before and communicates specific details of events

that won't unfold for hundreds of years. There would
be a Savior, born of a virgin,[24] called mighty God,[25]
who would give sight to the blind, open deaf ears, and
make the lame walk again.[26] He would be preceded by
a messenger crying out in the wilderness to prepare the
way of the Lord.[27] This Savior would be despised and
rejected by men.[28] He would remain silent before his
accusers[29] as they mocked him, beat him, spit on him,
and ripped parts of his beard out.[30] In chapter 53 the
words almost leap from the page:

> *Yet it was our weaknesses he carried;*
> *it was our sorrows that weighed him down.*
> *And we thought his troubles were a punishment from God,*
> *a punishment for his own sins!*
> *But he was pierced for our rebellion,*
> *crushed for our sins.*
> *He was beaten so we could be whole.*
> *He was whipped so we could be healed.*
> *All of us, like sheep, have strayed away.*
> *We have left God's paths to follow our own.*

---

24. Isaiah 7:14

25. Isaiah 9:6

26. Isaiah 35:4–6

27. Isaiah 40:3–5

28. Isaiah 53:1–3

29. Isaiah 53:7

30. Isaiah 50:6

Yet the LORD laid on him
the sins of us all. (Isaiah 53:4–6 NLT)

God was sending a Redeemer. The idea of a God-man paying for the sins of the world with His own life was not even a concept that existed at this point in history. What Isaiah was describing broke every man-made paradigm and construct in existence. God with flesh on, humiliated and murdered for the ransom of His creation? The rescue plan, despite the best (or worst) efforts of the world He was trying to save, was moving forward as planned. These words were written *hundreds of years* before Jesus Christ was born! Thanks to the Dead Sea Scrolls, we have actual physical copies of Isaiah that predate the birth of Christ by hundreds of years as well. It's a message of comfort, peace, and redemption sent to ease the great suffering of a nation that had rejected God, and a reminder that God had not abandoned His creation to their self-made suffering. It's hope in the form of prophecy. But there is something more here that I don't want us to miss. God, in all of His infinite wisdom, reaches through time to give us an incredible gift more than two thousand years after these words were written. He gives us a powerful reason to believe that the Bible is His Word, and He uses math.

One of the questions that has plagued every serious

thinker whose heart has been exposed to the truth of the Gospel is the following:

How can we know that the Bible is actually God's Word and not just a bunch of ancient writings by long-dead authors with an authority complex?

The answer to this question is multifaceted. There are many books available that discuss the answer to that question in great detail, so we are only going to scratch the surface here. In his book *Evidence That Demands a Verdict*, Josh McDowell writes that if God created man with a desire to know Him, we would expect His message to have some unique properties. Here are just the first three:

It would be widely distributed so man could attain it easily.

It would be preserved through time without corruption.

It would be completely accurate historically.

In all three of these categories the Bible shines. It is the most widely distributed piece of literature in history. Due to thousands of ancient pieces of manuscript evidence, is it arguably the most well-preserved and uncorrupted ancient document of all time. No other ancient text comes close. [31]

---

31. Josh McDowell, *The New Evidence that Demands a Verdict* (Nashville, TN: Thomas Nelson Publishers, 1999), 55.

Author	Book	Date Written	Earliest Copies	Time Gap	# of Copies
Homer	Iliad	800 BC	c. 400 BC	c. 400 yrs.	643
Herodotus	History	480–425 BC	c. AD 900	c. 1350 yrs.	8
Thucydides	History	460–400 BC	c. AD 900	c. 1300 yrs.	8
Plato		400 BC	c. AD 900	c. 1300 yrs.	7
Demosthenes		300 BC	c. AD 1100	c. 1400 yrs.	200
Caesar	Gallic Wars	100–44 BC	c. AD 900	c. 1000 yrs.	10
Livy	History of Rome	59 BC–AD 17	c. AD 400 (partial) c. AD 1000 (most)	c. 400 yrs. c. 1000 yrs.	1 (partial) 19
Tacitus	Annals	AD 100	c. AD 1100	c. 1000 yrs.	20
Pliny Secundus	Natural History	AD 61–113	c. AD 850	c. 750 yrs.	7
New Testament		AD 50–100	c. AD.114 (fragment) c. AD 200 (books) c. AD 250 (most of N.T.) c. AD 325 (complete N.T.)	c. +50 yrs. c. 100 yrs. c. 150 yrs. c. 225 yrs.	5366

32

---

32. Josh McDowell, *The New Evidence that Demands a Verdict* (Nashville, TN: Thomas Nelson Publishers, 1999), 38.

There are also many written sources outside the Bible that corroborate its documentation. The first-century historian Flavius Josephus, the Jewish Talmud, a Samaritan historian named Thallus who wrote in AD 52, and the Roman historian Phlegon are all sources that authenticate the historical accuracy of the Bible.

The Bible itself claims to be the written Word of God, but here is one of the most amazing evidences in support of that claim: fulfilled prophecy. This is where we rejoin Isaiah. The mathematical odds of a living human being foretelling the future so specifically and having every single one of his prophecies come true is absolutely astronomical. The prophecies are not just limited to Isaiah. In Psalm 22, David predicts the crucifixion of Jesus, far before this method of execution was even devised and put to use by the Persians, Greeks, and then Romans. There are over three hundred specific prophecies of Jesus alone that were fulfilled during His lifetime. This isn't just highly mathematically improbable; it's nigh impossible. It would be along the lines of getting struck by lightning and winning the lottery. . .every day of your life. Fulfilled prophecy like this simply doesn't happen, unless the God of the Bible is real and working behind the scenes to advance His rescue plan for humankind. In the end, prophecy, like so many other things God uses, is really all about fixing our broken perspective. God is still God, no matter what the circumstance. He is still in control. He still loves us. We may not see it. We may not feel His presence, but our senses, or lack thereof, do not change eternal truth. He is still working out His rescue plan.

#HopeUnchained

The stench was unbearable at first, but after a few days, it slowly became the new normal. Squalor and filth were everywhere. These were not the modern prisons we know today. These were merely holding pens for people who had angered Herod, the ruler set in place by the Roman Empire. Waiting to die in a dirty prison, John the Baptist was beginning to lose hope. Had he wasted his life eating bugs and living off the grid for a fraud? Was this teacher from Galilee merely a teacher and nothing more? Had the Messiah he had clung to so fervently abandoned him? With nothing to do but sit in his cell and think, questions plagued him unrelentingly. Years ago, when he had been a child, his mother had recounted the incredible story of his birth. She'd told him how the angel had come to his father as he performed his priestly duties in the temple, and how his dad couldn't quite wrap his mind around the good news of the special son that would be born. She'd smiled as she talked about the quiet house in the months of her pregnancy and his father's inability to speak due to the angelic curse. That particular subject seemed to come up quite a bit actually, usually during marital disagreements, he remembered with a grin. He remembered his parents teaching him about the special promises God had asked of him, to set him apart for a very special purpose. He was to be the messenger announcing the coming of the Messiah. *The Messiah!* For thousands of years they had waited for their prophesied savior to arrive. He remembered the story of his cousin's birth in a stable during the great census and shook his head in disbelief. What a strange way for the Messiah to come. He thought about the years he'd spent in the wilderness, the crowds that would flock to hear him and be baptized, and his message to anyone who would listen: "Get ready! The Lord is coming!" It all seemed so distant now, and his wrists and ankles ached inside the shackles that now bound him. Was this all simply a colossal misunderstanding? His cell door creaked open, and John winced as the light hit his eyes. He had grown accustomed to the darkness, and the bright light of day was painful. He could make out a lone figure in the doorway, and as the figure drew near, he breathed a sigh of relief. It was one of his disciples. Earlier in the day he had sent him out with a message for Jesus: "Are you the Messiah we've been expecting, or should we keep looking for someone else?" His disciple hurriedly whispered the Messiah's response.

"Go back to John and tell him what you have heard

and seen—the blind see, the lame walk, those with leprosy are cured, the deaf hear, the dead are raised to life, and the Good News is being preached to the poor." And he added, 'God blesses those who do not fall away because of me.'" (Matthew 11:3–6 NLT)

Perspective. It was exactly what John needed, and his Savior knew it. The situation seemed dire, even hopeless. John's eyes were clouded by the darkness of pain and discouragement, and the One who opened the eyes of the blind peeled back the layers of despair to allow truth to flood in. He didn't change the situation. There were no broken chains or crumbling cell walls, but in an instant John was free from the prison in his own mind. God's rescue plan was moving forward, and all the strength of the Roman army itself could not have stopped this cosmic force of hope and redemption. He didn't know how, or when, but somehow he knew that the Messiah would make all things right, and that was all he needed to hear.

He was not abandoned.

#LostandFound

Surrounded by fluffy farm animals, the boy sat quietly sobbing. He felt utterly alone. Through his tears, the boy felt a familiar hand on his shoulder. Startled, he turned to see the face of his father looking down at him. "Are you all right, buddy?" There were no words. The boy buried his face in his dad's arms. "I've been here the whole time. Didn't you hear me calling?" The little boy shook his head. It didn't matter now.

He was not abandoned.

Chapter 6

#UnconventionalHero

It is not great faith, but true faith, that saves; and the salvation lies not in the faith, but in the Christ in whom faith trusts.

—Charles Haddon Spurgeon, *All of Grace*

A thick haze of pulverized concrete and acrid smoke from the scorched wreckage stung her eyes and burned her lungs as she timidly made her way across the deserted street to the dilapidated diner. A blackened husk lay in the road where a late-model sedan had once been. She gripped the hand of her little brother tightly and pulled him along behind her. The screeching roars that had been getting ever-closer were now eerily silent. She brushed back the auburn wisps of hair from her soot-covered face and pushed on the diner's broken front door with all the might left in her twelve-year-old body. The metal frame groaned and gave way slightly, opening just enough for her and her weary brother to slip through the narrow opening. Sunlight filtered through the dust-covered windows of the old eatery, casting pale yellow beams of light across an empty room filled with the broken remnants of what had been a thriving diner just days ago. "Marta, I'm hungry," the small boy whimpered. She looked down at her brother, who had discovered an empty box of crackers and was busy shaking it into his open mouth in a vain attempt to catch crumbs that didn't exist. She reached down to tussle his hair and surveyed their new environment for possible food options. "Wait here," she instructed him. "I'll check the kitchen." Three steps later, she realized her mistake. As the door to the kitchen swung open, she froze, her eyes locked with two glowing red orbs imbedded in the face of a creature escaped from the nightmares of a madman. Its black, sinewy body stiffened, and it rose from whatever poor object it had previously been intent on devouring to focus its full attention on her. It had been tracking them since early this morning, and now the hunter had cornered its prey. There was nowhere to run, nowhere to hide. With blinding speed, the creature leapt at her. Stumbling back, she fell with her head buried in her hands waiting for the terrible impact. It never came.

A deafening crash forced her eyes open. To her amazement, she saw her attacker lying lifeless on the floor in front of her, under a rather large, newly opened hole in the ceiling. Her brother stood in the doorway, his mouth agape.

"It was him," he gasped, "the [Insert Random Superhero Name Here]."

#SuperObsession

From hulking green behemoths of unlimited strength to the flowing red capes and shiny tights that no normal human would ever consider fashionably appropriate, we are a culture obsessed with superheroes. Faster, stronger, smarter, and tougher than any mere mortal, these champions of virtue are a personification of all the potential for good that we see in ourselves. As a culture, we love the idea of amazing, yet sometimes flawed protectors, swooping in to save us in our moment of desperation. The concept sells movie tickets like none other. In fact, from 2012 to 2015, over eighteen new superhero blockbusters launched onto the big screen, resulting in over $10 billion in ticket sales.[33] That's *billion*, with a *B*. This figure doesn't even include sales from all the T-shirts, action figures, video games, and other merchandising.

In our superhero-obsessed culture, it's telling that the biblical character with the most superhuman powers was also one of the biggest failures. His name was Samson. Strength, speed, and power are the perceived

---

33. *Wikipedia*, s.v. "List of American Superhero Films," last modified July 19. 2017, http://en.wikipedia.org/wiki/List_of_American_superhero_films.

way to greatness in our eyes, but God had something different in mind with His rescue plan.

#OriginStory

Four hundred years had passed in silence. The descendants of Abraham had learned an excruciating lesson in their time of exile. The remnant had returned to rebuild and start over. Malachi had been the last prophet whom God had used to communicate with His people. They were looking for the promised Messiah, a deliverer sent to once again free them from bondage, and they needed it now. Their homeland fell to the Greeks in 333 BC, and ten years later, it fell to the Egyptians. Their new overlords were not all bad, and Jews were largely treated well in those days. They adopted the Greek language and many of the customs.

Everything crumbled when Antiochus the Great of Syria captured the land in 204 BC. Both he and his successor, Antiochus Epiphanes, persecuted the chosen people, and in 171 BC Epiphanes desecrated the Holy of Holies by sacrificing a pig on the altar. This defilement resulted in an armed uprising led by Judas Maccabeus, and in 165 BC the Jews recaptured Jerusalem. They continued to fight with the Syrians until the Romans conquered their homeland in 63 BC, when Caesar set up his two sons as rulers over the area. As the New Testament opens, one of these sons, Herod the Great, is bearing down on God's people and strengthening his grip on power in the region. After all this time, a voice cries out in the wilderness, "Prepare the way of the Lord!" The silence is finally broken.

Let me be clear: the Jews *were* looking for a savior. They desperately wanted someone who could help them break free from the bonds of the Roman Empire. They wanted a great warrior, a powerful leader who could crush their enemies under his fist and bring prosperity and recognition to a nation bruised and weary from years of suffering. They had no idea their real need for deliverance was far more significant. Like the man who walked into the doctor's office to clear up some troublesome asthma, only to discover that his lungs were filled with stage four cancer, Abraham's children wanted deliverance from a temporal trouble when their real issue was eternal separation from their Creator. They were looking for a savior; they just didn't recognize the One they needed when He finally broke onto the scene one night in the humblest of ways. Born in a barn and laid in a feeding trough for livestock, the Rescuer of the world had come. Shepherds, one of the lowest professions of the Jewish social order, were present to welcome God Himself. For thousands of years the world had waited—but they had no idea what was coming.

Jesus grew up in the house of a carpenter. He was likely familiar with hard work. From what we can gather in the Bible, His childhood was much like the upbringing of any other boy at the time, save His flight to Egypt as a toddler to escape a wicked king bent on His slaughter, and a short account of a few days spent in the temple as a tween, doing His Father's work.[34] There was no grand entrance, no parade or lavish gala announcing the arrival of the most important figure to tread the dirt of the planet since its creation. Sure, there were hosts of angels singing at his birth, but they had appeared to shepherds, not foreign dignitaries or people with great influence and power. There were no flowing red capes or stretchy tights. There was no flashy uniform or powerful entourage. There was no cool superhero name or fancy chariot emblazoned with His logo. He was, for all practical purposes, just a normal guy, but there was much more to Him than met the eye.

#TheTalk

A simple conversation was all he wanted, just a few minutes with the man behind the movement. The news of His arrival had swept through the city like a wildfire. This man, a simple carpenter by trade, spoke with authority unlike any that had come before Him. The Wildman in

---

34. Luke 2:41–52

the Wilderness had proclaimed Him to be the Messiah, the saving One that all of Israel had been waiting for. There had been other self-proclaimed Messiahs but none that performed signs and miracles like Jesus, none that spoke with His certainty and conviction. He had singlehandedly driven the greedy vultures from the temple courtyard that preyed upon the worshippers who gathered there. His eyes had flashed as He drove the scavengers and their livestock out, flipping tables and scattering coins into the dust. "Get these things out of here! How dare you turn My Father's house into a common flea market!"[35] He shouted through the chaos, yet His kindness and compassion for the poor and vulnerable were a refreshing summer breeze through the stale, choking haze of religious regulation and ritual that Nicodemus had become so accustomed to over the years. This man was out to impress no one. He wasn't playing by the rules of politics and power mongering that everyone else was. He spoke openly of repentance and forgiveness. He spoke of the kingdom of God. He spent time with the "untouchables" of His day—outcasts and misfits that society and the religious elite refused to even acknowledge. He was different. Nicodemus was determined to speak with Him, but it was far too risky to be associated with such a radical in the light of day.

The sun had set when they finally got a chance to

---

35. John 2:16

meet. Glad for the cover of darkness, Nicodemus slipped away to secretly go to the place Jesus was staying. His mind was brimming with questions, but he thought it wise to start with a compliment: "We all know God has sent you to teach us. Your miracles are proof enough that God is with you." The Messiah's response caught him by surprise and cut through his carefully manicured facade of religiosity.

"Unless you are born again, you can never see the kingdom of God."

What! What on earth was He talking about? Maybe this man was more than a little crazy. Did He honestly expect a full-grown man to crawl back inside the womb of his mother? Jesus had pierced through the thin veneer of this law-abiding Pharisee, straight to the heart of the matter. Nicodemus' culture was obsessed with self-righteousness. He believed that if he could be good enough and follow the laws, do the right things, and give to the right causes, he might somehow earn God's favor and fix the rift between God and humankind that had existed since the garden. Nicodemus had fallen for the big lie. This is the gospel of humanity—that given enough time and effort, man can somehow atone for his own sin. He can repair the break in the relationship himself. In the next few words, Jesus obliterated that false gospel like a baseball bat through a crystal vase and sent the shards of Nicodemus' theology spinning into the crisp night air.

Jesus replied, "I assure you, no one can enter the Kingdom of God without being born of water and the Spirit. . . . For this is how God loved the world: He gave His one and only Son, so that everyone who believes in him will not perish but have eternal life. God sent his Son into the world not to judge the world, but to save the world through him." (John 3:5, 16–17 NLT)

It was never about what humanity could do. All the hard work and rule following in the world could never accomplish what Jesus came to do. After years spent enslaved to ritual and religion, Nicodemus came to the slow realization that pride had been at the root of it all. As Nicodemus struggled to comprehend this new idea, his mind reeled with the claims of the man sitting across from him. He called Himself God.[36] He spoke not only of judgment but of redemption. The Messiah had come not to rescue him from others but to save him from himself. This changed everything.

Jesus Christ had not come to destroy the law. He had not come to help people follow it better and thereby earn God's favor. He came to do what no one else could: follow it perfectly. Every single line and every single letter of the law was kept flawlessly by the Messiah, even down

---

36. John 3:13

to the thoughts in His head and the motives in His heart. Love God. Love others. That's what Christ did, and He did it to perfection. Time after time the religious leaders of the day attempted to trip Him up with trick questions and verbal barbs, but each time He answered perfectly. "Who do you think you are?" they protested. Jesus' answer in John 8:56–59 is stunning:

> "Your father Abraham rejoiced as he looked forward to my coming. He saw it and was glad." The people said, "You aren't even fifty years old. How can you say you have seen Abraham?" Jesus answered, "I tell you the truth, before Abraham was even born, I AM!" At that point they picked up stones to throw at him. But Jesus was hidden from them and left the Temple. (NLT)

I AM. We know that name. It was how the Infinite had introduced Himself to an outcast in the desert hundreds of years before. Jesus was not merely a great teacher. He wasn't just an admirable historical figure with a message of peace and hope for the world. He wasn't simply a moral person who advocated for social justice. He called Himself God, and the religious elites of the day knew exactly what He had said. They were so angry and offended that they tried to murder Him on the spot, but it wasn't time for that yet.

In a culture where children were to be seen and not

heard, Jesus made time for the youngest. He went out of His way to talk with a Samaritan woman at a well, in a society where women were considered to be second-class citizens, and Samaritans were lower in social stature than dogs. He had no time for the nonsensical social rules and arbitrary classes that people had created in order to gain power and wealth at the cost of others. He was and is compassion personified and love displayed. Jesus fed the hungry, healed the sick, gave sight to the blind, and gave the gift of hearing to the deaf. He grieved over the deep spiritual pain of Jerusalem and wept openly at the death of a friend, yet in the face of danger and overwhelming peril, He soldiered forward with courage and strength unmatched in the whole of human history.

#GhostontheWater

The sea crashed in the darkness, as if it were a great monster bent on devouring the ship. The sailors were terrified. They were no strangers to the sea, and each one knew all too well how this night could end. The cold blackness enveloped them like a funeral shroud. Waves relentlessly pounded the small fishing boat, each one more immense than the last. The unyielding wind had caught them all by surprise, even though some of them had spent their whole lives on these waters. *I knew this was a mistake*, Peter had thought, but he'd obeyed anyway and obediently launched out into the Sea of Galilee, just as his Master had ordered. This wasn't the first time he'd endured bad weather at sea, but something was ominously different tonight. It was two hours past midnight, and the clouds that blocked the moonlight created an eerie pall over the surging sea. The men on the boat strained against the force of the squall, fighting to keep their little craft afloat. Why did Jesus have to pick such a poor time to leave them alone? He felt so much safer with Him. No matter the social pressure or the constant threat of harm or even death from the enemies of the Way, Peter trusted his Master. Jesus had never let him down. Peering through the night, one of them saw something, a shape moving on the waves, and cried out in alarm! He cried out to the others, waving his arms and pointing. As it drew nearer, a hush fell over the men. The form on the water was not a boat. It was a man, or something like it. There, in the distance, was a hazy figure approaching them in the darkness. Peter's blood ran as cold as the sea water that threatened to drag them all to its murky depths. The ghostly apparition moved quickly over the water toward their sinking vessel. Fear gripped the men, snatching the very breath from their lungs. Frozen in wide-eyed terror, they could barely believe what they were seeing. He'd heard stories of specters like this, ghosts of vengeful sailors taken by the sea, but always quickly dismissed them as old wives' tales. He wiped his disbelieving eyes with his sleeve and looked again. It was undeniable. There was something—*someone* there, and it was getting closer. Panic struck the boat, and grown men screamed in terror at the specter that bore down on their vessel. Suddenly, a voice like a thunderclap echoed across the water. They knew it well. The God of the universe in human form was on His way to rescue them.

"It's all right. I am here. Don't be afraid."

It sounded just like the Master. Peter's head was spinning now. The turbulent sea wasn't helping any. Fear and disbelief melted into amazement. Could it really be Him? His heart pounded as if it would break free from his chest.

"Lord, if it is really You, tell me to come to You by walking on the water!"

Peter was a doer, not an overthinker. Fear raced through Peter's mind, but Christ's answer came like a stick in the spokes of a speeding bicycle.

"All right, come."

Gingerly, Peter stepped over the side of the boat onto the tumultuous water. His foot found firm support, and he started making his way to the Savior *walking on the water*! He could hardly believe it. *How was this possible?* It almost felt like a dream, until the cold spray of reality from the waves jarred him back into the moment. His eyes strayed from his Master to the crashing water and darkness that threatened to swallow him completely. What was he thinking? This was a terrible idea. He gasped as the cold water started to envelop his feet, then legs. He started to panic. The fear came flooding back as he started to sink. "Save me, Lord!" he cried out. Almost before the words had left his lips, a hand clasped firmly around his own.

"Why did you doubt Me?"

Fear clouds faith. The Savior of the world had reached out to save one man, not just from a watery grave, but from fear itself.[37]

What is the true measure of a hero? Is it strength or courage? Is it the ability to do what no one else can or the vision to see danger and know how to react? Is it simply the will to act when no one else will? Perhaps, but I would say that one of the most defining characteristics of a hero is the ability to put others' needs ahead of their own, even at their own peril.

#NotMyWill

It was getting late, and the next few days were going to be treacherous, but Jesus had gathered them here for a reason. The Passover feast was over. This time felt different than any Passover before it. Jesus spoke of many things that night, and the confused disciples had trouble grasping why He kept talking about leaving them. Their Messiah

---

37. Matthew 14

spoke of sending a Helper and told them that the world would hate them just as it hated Him. These certainly were not the words of someone about to overthrow the Roman oppression. When Jesus gave them bread and wine, He asked them to remember His body and blood poured out for them.[38] *What was He talking about?* They had no idea that Jesus was about to embark on the most grueling few days since the dawn of humanity—and that He was doing it for them. If there were ever a time that someone deserved to be inwardly focused, it was now. In John 13–16, we see Jesus consumed with preparing His followers as best He could for His upcoming absence. When under immense personal stress, Jesus Christ chose to put others before Himself. He knew the grueling task ahead of Him and still had the humility and grace to think of His disciples. The greatest testament to this is found in chapter 17. In that passage, we see one of the most extraordinary prayers recorded in Scripture. Jesus prays for *us.* The night before the worst agony ever experienced would be inflicted upon our Savior, He prayed for you and for me. He prays first for the will of God to be done, and that His glory would be shown. He prays for God to keep and care for His disciples, but in verses 20 and 21, in the middle of all the stress and pressure of the impending crucifixion, Jesus prays this:

> *"I am praying not only for these disciples but also for*

38. Matthew 26

all who will ever believe in me through their message. I pray that they will all be one, just as you and I are one—as you are in me, Father, and I am in you. And may they be in us so that the world will believe you sent me." (NLT)

Unbelievable. A true hero has the ability to put others' needs ahead of their own, and Christ does this flawlessly here, and at His own peril. The pieces of God's costly, divine rescue plan were falling into place.

#AGriefObserved

Watching His son walk up the mountain was the hardest part. The wood that He carried on His back would soon be used in His death. He had done nothing to deserve this. His only son, the fulfillment of a long-awaited promise, was now walking toward the impending doom that awaited Him at the end of the journey. Few people know the agony of losing a child, but like Abraham of old on his way up the side of Mt. Moriah, God understood it perfectly.

God will provide a way out.

Who could have predicted that the way out would be *this*? As God watched Abraham's pain in obedience, He knew from experience what it felt like. I AM, the infinite, timeless God of the universe, had already experienced

His own Son walking that heartrending path, carrying the wood that would be used to crucify Him. Christ had done nothing to deserve death. By the miracle of His virgin birth, He had escaped the taint of sin that stained every other human born on this planet. He met every mark set by God. He kept the whole law, down to the very last letter. If the payment for sin is death, He alone deserved life—but God watched as the long-awaited fulfillment of the promised Messiah stumbled toward impending doom.

This was the Way out.

This was the Passover lamb, sacrificed to save others. Jesus was the rescue plan. God in flesh took the punishment that we deserved on Himself, so that we could be restored to God. He never meant for Abraham to kill his own son. That was a task far too heartrending, too excruciating for anyone to be asked to do. No one should be asked to give up their only son as a sacrifice, but God had a rescue plan, and He would stop at nothing to see it through. No pain was too great. No price was too high. No sacrifice was too much to rescue the creation He so deeply loved, so He continued with His plan and provided a substitute. Sacrificial true love won out over self-preservation. Isaac lived. Jesus died. The Hero put the needs of the entire world ahead of His own, at the cost of His life.

#FatalFinale

Marta rummaged quickly through the remnants of the old diner's kitchen, hoping to find something edible. The encounter moments before had left her shaken, but unscathed. Every few seconds her eyes involuntarily darted back to the dark heap that lay lifeless on the floor where her attacker had once stood, scanning for any sign of movement. Little Hector was beside her now, his hand holding tightly to her shirt. She knew that they needed food soon, and it was up to her to find it. Scattered, empty boxes and broken dishes littered the floor. Finally, in a metal cupboard that had been hidden behind a collapsed section of the wall, she found her prize—a small stash of canned fruit that had been missed by the previous scavengers who had raided the diner for supplies. She cleared away the debris from a corner of the diner's main eatery and set out their feast. The yellow beams of light filtering through the dusty windows had begun to turn orange as the sun sank lower in the sky. Without a sound, her little brother shoveled the treasure into his mouth. She had never seen him this hungry, and it was good to finally be able to watch him eat.

Suddenly, his head snapped up in alarm, his eyes wide with fear. "Look!" he choked, his cheeks still stuffed with the peaches he'd been devouring seconds before. There in the street, a black silhouette skittered through the long shadows of dusk. It was not alone. Another emerged from its hiding place briefly, before disappearing into the darkness of an alleyway just across the street. As Marta watched, a great wave of dread washed over her. She realized they were surrounded by not one or two, but hundreds of the same type of foul creature that they had been rescued from earlier. There was no escape this time. A loud shriek jarred her back to her senses. It was her little brother, but this was no cry of terror. He was cheering and pointing at a blur of light in the street. Their savior had returned! Dark fiends converged on their would-be rescuer like hungry wolves. Flashes of light erupted from the writhing mass of chaos. Black husks were sent hurtling through the air, but for every monster that the hero slew, three more joined the fray. In one final, brilliant explosion, the mass of dark hunters went flying back from the force of the blast. When the dust cleared, Marta lifted her head to survey the wreckage. There in the street lay their hope, their hero, dead. The stunned creatures re-gathered themselves and converged on the body with renewed ferocity.

End scene.

Credits roll.

Worst. Rescue. Ever.

What producer of a superhero blockbuster in their right mind would end a movie like that? The hero can't die! What about the rescue plan? What about the hope and salvation of the world? I'm sure that the disciples of Christ had similar questions as they stood looking at the torn, bloody, and battered corpse of the Man they thought was their Messiah. Death wins?

Chapter 7

#TheDifference

If Jesus rose from the dead, then you have to accept all that he said; if he didn't rise from the dead, then why worry about any of what he said? The issue on which everything hangs is not whether or not you like his teaching but whether or not he rose from the dead.

—Timothy J. Keller, *The Reason for God: Belief in an Age of Skepticism*

The afternoon rain fell steadily on the field, now well-worn from the feet of the hundreds of gaunt figures that huddled together. Days of relentless rainfall had taken their toll, and the field was now more of a swamp than anything else. The legs of the scattered crowd were mud caked, and the light, ragged clothing they wore did little to ward off the chilling rain. A few whispered in guarded tones as others glanced about nervously, never raising their heads, trying not to draw unwanted attention. To the south rose several lines of long, ramshackle buildings, as bleak and unwelcoming as the dark gray sky they silhouetted. As far as the eye could see, tall barbed-wire fences and intimidating wooden guard towers enclosed the compound. A cloud of despair hung heavy and thick over the Cabanatuan prison camp.

"I'm not exactly sure how much longer I can do this," whispered one of the shadowy forms to three others that crouched beside him. His voice cracked with emotion, and his eyes slipped closed in desperation. The others nodded sympathetically, layers of dirt and grime on their faces unable to mask the hopelessness that they, too, felt. A lone figure slowly approached them and placed his hand on the shoulder of one of the men.

"Good news," he said quietly. "The Yanks are pushing hard, and news from the front is that something secret is in the works. They just brought in a few more badly wounded, and one of them managed to speak to me before they carted him off."

"Good news," scoffed one of the men in a torn linen shirt. He shuddered as the wind whipped, and he pushed his hands deeper into his pockets. "I've heard that same story more times than I can count. MacArthur and his forces have all returned to Luzon. We are on our own now. We'll all be dead of starvation or the elements before anyone reaches us."

"Or something worse," muttered another. "Nobody ever

gets out of here, but for the corpses on the wagons. There is no escape, save death. Ain't nobody comin' for us now."

#NoEscape

Death is the great equalizer. It comes to the rich and poor alike. It has no regard for wealth, political power, or social standing, and the greatest minds in history have succumbed to its inevitable dominion. Though we spend incredible amounts of our time and resources trying to delay it, no one escapes its grasp. Death comes to us all.

It had not always been this way. In the garden, humankind was given a choice—obey the simple command given by the Creator and choose life, or disobey with deadly consequences. It's not hard to guess which path was taken. Since then, humanity has mourned the loss of our friends and loved ones as time marches forward. We all are forced to face our own mortality at some point. Through the years, many have devised theories of what happens to the part of us that thinks, feels, and is self-aware after we die. Some would call that part a soul. Popular ideas gained traction, and influential people developed followers based on the teachings of these ideas. It was humanity's attempt at fixing the problem of death, a rescue plan forged by their own hand, a collection of humanist gospels. At their best, they were only theory crafters. No one had been to the other side of death and come back to verify whether any of the ideas were true. This is a summary of every single world religion. This is the best we can do on our own. This is where the Gospel stands apart from the crowd. One Man did die, stayed dead for three days, and returned to life. One Man went to the other side and came back to give hope to all others. One Man broke through the impenetrable, escaped the inescapable, and defeated the overwhelming power of the grave. That Man was God in human form, Jesus Christ.

What sets the Gospel apart from the rest of the world's beliefs? The resurrection of Christ. While we were helpless and destined for eternal death, He overcame the grave, and in Acts 1:3 it says that Jesus "presented Himself alive after His suffering, by many convincing proofs" (NASB). What are these convincing proofs that Luke is writing about? Here is an attempt to show some of these proofs and their profound effect on the way we view the resurrection of Jesus Christ. These proofs do not require one to believe that the Bible is anything other than a historically accurate collection of men's writings, which most scholars would easily concede, and for good reason as we saw in chapter 4. I owe a lot of this research to a graduate professor of mine, Dr. Gary Habermas. He challenged me to think critically about the resurrection.

Buckle up. We are about to head into one of the most incredible events in all of history.

Ten Historical Facts Accepted by Virtually All Scholars

1. Jesus' Death by Crucifixion

Crucifixion by Roman executioners might be one of the most excruciating deaths known to man. Suffocation is the mode by which life is slowly extracted. Here is a summary of an article in *The Journal of the American Medical Association* on March 21, 1986, Volume 256.

> *Jesus of Nazareth underwent Jewish and Roman trials, was flogged, and was sentenced to death by crucifixion. The scourging produced deep stripe like lacerations and appreciable blood loss, and it probably set the stage for hypovolemic shock, as evidenced by the fact that Jesus was too weakened to carry the crossbar (patibulum) to Golgotha. At the site of crucifixion, his wrists were nailed to the patibulum and, after the patibulum was lifted onto the upright post (stipes), his feet were nailed to the stipes. The major pathophysiologic effect of crucifixion was an interference with normal respirations. Accordingly, death resulted primarily from hypovolemic shock and exhaustion asphyxia. Jesus' death was ensured*

by the thrust of a soldier's spear into his side. Mod-
ern medical interpretation of the historical evidence
indicates that Jesus was dead when taken down from
the cross.[39]

It was a common occurrence for the Roman executioners to break the legs of the victims if they were taking too long to die. These soldiers were in the business
of killing condemned men, and they were masters of
their trade. They had good reason to be. *Fustuarium* was
the term for the penalty of death that Roman soldiers
received if they failed to carry out their duties. It was a
severe form of military punishment in which a soldier
was beaten to death with clubs by his fellow soldiers,
sometimes in the form of running a gauntlet. Considering the fact that if someone survived an execution by
crucifixion, it would cost the executioners their lives, it
is highly unlikely that a whole squad of executioners
could miss someone who was not completely dead. One
of the tests to confirm the demise of the condemned
was a well-placed spear into the pericardial cavity of the
human body. When the soldiers saw the fluid and blood
run from the wound, they could see that the heart had
been pierced by their spear, confirming the death of the
condemned.

---

39. W. D. Edwards, W. J. Gabel, and F. E. Hosmer, "On the Physical Death of Jesus
Christ." *JAMA.* 255 no. 11 (1986):1455–1463, doi:10.1001
/jama.1986.03370110077025.

2. Jesus' Burial

There is relatively no argument about the fact that Jesus was buried in a family tomb owned by Joseph of Arimathea. Not only did Joseph bury Christ, but Pilate also sealed the tomb with the Roman seal of authority and set a Roman guard unit to stand watch over it to prevent foul play. A large stone was rolled against the entrance. It was customary to roll big stones against tombs to keep would-be thieves or wildlife from stealing valuables or defiling the corpse. These stones were generally too big to be moved by just a few men, so levers were used to move them. Some have estimated that the stone that sealed Jesus' tomb weighed one and a half to two tons, which is the approximate weight of a midsize car.[40] A Roman seal, comprised of a rope slung across the surface of the stone, and attached to the sides of the tomb wall, would have been fastened as well at the order of Pilate, to warn away robbers. The punishment for defacing a Roman seal was death, carried out by being crucified upside down. This seal was conspicuously missing when the empty tomb was discovered. This Roman guard unit was also under the Roman discipline method of *Fustuarium*, so keep in mind they were guarding this tomb with their lives. This guard was most likely an elite unit of sixteen

---

40. Justin Taylor, "What Did Jesus' Tomb Look Like?: An Interview with Leen Ritmeyer," *The Gospel Coalition* (blog), July 24, 12008, http://www.thegospel coalition.org/blogs/justintaylor/2008/07/24/what-did-jesus-tomb-look-like-interview/.

"commandos" from the best-trained, most well-equipped army in the world, placed under the authority of Pilate, the governor of the Roman province of Judea from AD 26 until around AD 36.[41]

3. The Despair of the Disciples

The disciples were clearly thrown into chaos and despair at the death of their Messiah, whom they most likely expected to lead a successful revolution against the Roman Empire. These men had seen some incredible things in their time with Jesus, but nothing prepared them for the shock of His death. They immediately went into hiding for fear of their own lives.

4. The Tomb Was Actually Empty

If the tomb was not empty, the Jewish leaders and the Roman government would have quickly retrieved the body for all to see to quell the enormous movement during Pentecost. They went to great lengths and spent a great deal of money trying to silence the story that Christ had been raised from the dead but were completely unable to do so.[42]

5. The Disciples' Eyewitness Accounts

The disciples genuinely believed that they had seen the risen Christ, even though some, like Thomas, did not wish to believe. How do we know that they truly believed that they had seen the risen Savior? Check out the next fact.

41. Matthew 27:57–66
42. Matthew 28:11–15; Acts 4:1–2

6. The Transformation of the Disciples

They were willing to be butchered for their faith. Early church tradition is the source of much of our information on the deaths of the apostles. Eusebius, one of the most important early church historians, wrote in AD 325 that the apostles and disciples of the Savior scattered over the whole world and preached the Gospel everywhere. In 1563, an English historian named John Foxe wrote an account entitled *Actes and Monuments*, a book that later became the more widely known *Foxe's Book of Martyrs*. In it, he recounted the history of some of their deaths.[43]

- Bartholomew, Simon the Zealot, Jude, (commonly called Thaddeus), Philip, Andrew, and Peter were all crucified in various ways.
- Luke was hanged from an olive tree in Greece.
- Matthew suffered martyrdom in Ethiopia, killed by a halberd, or a long, bladed pole-type weapon.
- Mark was dragged by horses through the streets until he was dead in Alexandria.
- John was boiled alive in a huge basin of boiling oil during a wave of persecution in Rome, but did not die. He was then banished to the island of Patmos, where he penned the book of Revelation.

43. John Foxe, *Foxe's Book of Martyrs* (Grand Rapids: Zondervan, 1967), 3–5.

- James, the brother of Christ and the leader of the church in Jerusalem, was beaten to death at age 94 in Jerusalem.
- James the Greater, a son of Zebedee, was beheaded in Jerusalem.
- Thomas was impaled with a spear in India.
- Even the apostle Paul, who penned the book of Romans on which #*Gospel* is based, was tortured and then beheaded after spending years as a Roman prisoner.

These men gave their lives in some of the most gruesome and painful ways imaginable. Why would anyone ever endure torture and death if by just admitting the fraud they would be set free?

7. The Disciples' Preaching in Jerusalem at the Epicenter of the Resurrection

It is one thing to try to pass off a lie as truth two thousand years and thousands of miles removed from where it happened. It is another thing entirely to do it in an environment where people had firsthand knowledge of the event and could easily go check on the facts themselves.

8. Birth of the Christian Church

The fact that the movement created by the resurrection still exists today is substantial, considering its combination with all the other proofs. There are many world religions that have large, even worldwide followings, but none that boast a resurrected Savior supported by evidence.

9. Migration from Saturday to Sunday Worship

In the letters of Paul to various churches, there was plenty of conflict concerning the Sabbath and Judaizers.[44] If Paul himself had introduced Sunday worship, he may have been accused of this in Acts 21:21 when he was accused of teaching against circumcision and against observing the customs. However, Paul was not specifically accused of teaching against Sabbath observance or promoting Sunday worship at the Jerusalem conference in Acts 15. It can be argued that Paul found the custom already established among Christians when he began his mission, which would indicate that the custom originated among Jewish Christians.[45] Saturday worship had centuries of tradition behind it, so there must have been an incredibly compelling reason to switch to Sunday, a reason like the miraculous resurrection of Jesus Christ.

10. James' (the Brother of Jesus) Conversion

Who would know the deep, dark secrets of your past better than a brother or sister? James grew up with Jesus. He knew everything and still resisted the idea that his older brother was the Messiah. It wasn't until the resurrection that his heart was changed, when he saw his resurrected brother with his own eyes!

---

44. Galatians 4:10; Colossians 2:16–17; Romans 14:5–6; 1 Corinthians 16:2

45. Thomas C. Hanson, "The Origins of Sunday Worship in the Christian Church," GCI.org, accessed July 19, 2017, https://www.gci.org/law/sabbath/hanson.

Even with all this evidence, there have been, and will always be, those who struggle with the reality of Christ's resurrection. In the face of all these facts, theories arise and are presented as a counterpoint in hopes of disproving one of the most significant historical events of all time. If we would truly understand the strength of the evidence for the resurrection, we must also examine these theories against it to see if they stand up to scrutiny.

Theories against the Resurrection

1. Fraud or Stolen Body Theories

A. The disciples stole the body.

There are a plethora of problems with this theory. First, the despair of the disciples seems odd if they had a plan to steal the body and stage a resurrection. Second, if the disciples had stolen the body, the perceived appearances of Christ after His death would not have had the effect in their lives that it did. No one dies for something they know is a lie. Why would anyone ever endure torture and death if by simply admitting the lie, they would be set free?

The Roman-based guard was not about to stand aside and let the disciples take the body. They would have been executed. These soldiers also would have slaughtered the disciples with ease. Elite troops versus a bunch of fisherman and a tax collector? My money is on the professional death dealers. If there had been a struggle, it would have been reported, and there would have been evidence of it that the Jewish religious leaders would have quickly brought to light during the days after the resurrection. The two-ton sealed stone in front also complicated matters in an attempted body-snatching escapade.

B. The women stole the body.

Unless these women were part of a secret ninja society with exemplary fighting and stealth skills, it is again unthinkable that they would have been able to deal with the Roman guard and the two-ton stone. The disciples also probably would have checked it out and not believed.

C. Joseph of Arimathea moved the body elsewhere.

Soldiers and Jewish leaders would not have sealed and guarded an empty tomb.

D. The Jewish leaders/soldiers took the body.

The Jewish leaders were the very ones trying to disprove the resurrection. The penalty for the soldiers again for dereliction of duty was death. If they had the body, they would have quickly produced it as proof that Christ did not rise from the grave.

2. Other Fraud/Tomb Theories

A. The women went to the wrong tomb.

The disciples/Jewish leaders would have quickly remedied that.

B. The swoon theory

This theory states that Jesus didn't really die on the cross. He just lost consciousness. There is really no possibility that Jesus was alive when He was removed from the cross. The Romans who carried out His execution were experts in the trade of death. It is crazy to think that an entire squad of Roman executioners could miss the fact that Jesus wasn't dead yet. His pierced pericardial cavity confirmed His demise. Let's not forget the executioners' penalty for failure was death. It's one thing to have a meeting with the boss for a failure at work; it's a whole different ballgame to face the Roman gauntlet. Even in the ridiculous event that somehow Jesus did make it to the tomb alive, He was in no condition to move a two-ton stone, beat down the elite Roman guard with His bare, nail-pierced hands, and then stage an escape.

C. Spontaneous combustion

The alternative theories for a resurrected Christ just keep getting more and more crazy at this point. This one assumes that His body just caught fire and burned up, leaving no trace or ashes. This is problematic for a myriad of reasons, one of which being that the burial wraps were intact. The stone was rolled away. The guard was gone. If Jesus' body had just spontaneously erupted into flame, no one probably would have ever even known, because no one would have opened the sealed tomb.

D. Wild speculation

What if some undiscovered "mutant bacteria" ate Jesus' body? What if some aliens came and stole His body? These things have no intrinsic plausibility. This means that there is no evidence supporting the existence of any of these things. Before one can use these as arguments, one must first prove that they exist.

Based on this evidence, we can have a clear assurance that Jesus Christ did, in fact, rise from the dead, just like He promised He would. There are entire books devoted to this very subject. This is the crux of Christian belief. Jesus did die. He was raised from the dead. The divine rescue plan, set in place from the dawn of humanity's sin problem, had finally been accomplished. This is the single most important event in all of history. Paul puts it best in his letter to Corinth:

And if Christ has not been raised, your faith is worthless; you are still in your sins. Then those also who have fallen asleep in Christ have perished. If we have hoped in Christ in this life only, we are of all men most to be pitied. (1 Corinthians 15:17–19 NASB)

#WhispersofHope

The whispers of the small group had drawn the attention of a few others by now, who had wandered over to see what the commotion was all about. It was rare to see anyone talking openly anymore. Noise brought attention from the guards, and attention from the guards brought pain. They had learned that lesson quickly.

"MacArthur is gone, and with him went our chance at freedom," one of the men said with a sigh. His gaunt features and malnourished frame made it clear that he had been a prisoner for quite some time. The others nodded in silent agreement. With each passing day, the dream of ever getting back to their homes, on the other side of the world from this dismal prison camp in the Philippines, grew to feel less and less possible. The stranger with the "good news" slowly reached into his pocket and then stretched out his hand into the center of the huddled group. As he opened his hand, an audible gasp erupted from the small crowd. There in his palm was a blue and gold diamond patch, evidence of hope in the form of the Sixth Ranger Battalion of the US Army.[46]

---

46. *Wikipedia*, s.v. "Raid at Cabanatuan," last modified July 14, 2017, http://en.wikipedia.org/wiki/Raid_at_Cabanatuan.

Chapter 8
#MissionImpossible

If man had his way, the plan of redemption would be an end-less and bloody conflict. In reality, salvation was bought not by Jesus' fist, but by His nail-pierced hands; not by muscles but by love; not by vengeance but by forgiveness; not by force but by sacrifice. Jesus Christ our Lord surrendered in order that He might win; He destroyed His enemies by dying for them and conquered death by allowing death to conquer Him.

—A. W. Tozer, *Preparing for Jesus' Return: Daily Live the Blessed Hope*

The soft hum of billions of bits of encrypted information flowing freely all around him filled his ears like a soothing symphony. The dark figure crouched over the oven hatch before pulling a long black rope from a hidden pouch and carefully tossing it into the hole. He glanced at his watch for only a second before he descended silently, every move meticulously practiced and planned. The prowler knew his window of opportunity was infinitesimally small, and his prize was guarded by a seemingly impenetrable labyrinth of security and armed sentries. The cable quickly slid through his gloved hands as he slipped through the unmoving blades of a giant ventilation fan. The server farm was a fortress, impenetrable both physically and digitally. However, the many cramped machines created a lot of heat, and the solution to that problem was his way in. It wasn't much of a weak point. A small tube filled with spinning blades sounded more like a food processor than an entry point at first. The Herculean task required just to get there was overwhelming. Razor-wire fences, guard dogs, trained snipers in watch towers, and plenty of high-tech cameras and motion detection surrounding the hidden secure facility ensured the safety of the content inside.

"Fox, do you copy!"

His heart jumped as his earpiece crackled to life. "Maintain radio silence," he whispered back firmly, trying to remain calm.

"Fox, something is very wrong. I'm losing control of. . ."

Silence. Fox's mind raced. *Losing control of what? What is wrong? What is happening?* Then he heard it—the ominous low hum of electric fan motors coming back online.

#AgainstAllOdds

We love a good story about someone defying the odds and achieving the unachievable. Something about beating back overwhelming darkness thrills us to our core.

We don't just see this plot in spy movie thrillers either—it's everywhere. "If you dream it, you can achieve it" is part of our increasingly global culture; but sometimes, no matter how hard you dream, work, or believe, failure is inevitable. It turns out that some missions truly are, in fact, impossible. As humans, we are all contaminated by sin, and as a result, death is ultimately inescapable. As Paul wrote in Romans 2, if God is truly a perfectly just judge, something we all at our very core desperately want Him to be, He cannot overlook sin. His law shows us the magnitude of our failure.

We all stand rightly condemned.

So what now?

There can only be two responses. Either we try to deal with the problem ourselves or we admit our utter inability to do so and recognize God's rescue plan as the only way forward. Let's dig into this concept.

Every world religion is based on the premise that a person can somehow affect his or her eternal/spiritual outcome by doing things. For instance, if I do enough good, I can be reincarnated as something better; or if I follow the five pillars, Allah will be pleased with me. If I go to church and give money to the poor and don't murder anyone, God won't be mad at me. If I respect my ancestors, they will bless me. If I kill this person and throw his body down the steps of this ancient pyramid, the gods will send rain on our crops and allow us to conquer our enemies. . . and on and on it goes. Whether your religion of choice is embarking on two-year mandatory missionary quests or channeling "thetans" for self-improvement, all of them are based on the concept that we can somehow deal with our own spiritual problem. We are the masters of our fate. We can pull ourselves up by our own spiritual bootstraps.

Here is the crazy part: the root of all world religions is really the root of humanism as well. Humanism focuses on the value of human beings and usually implies a non-theistic life stance centered on human agency, looking to the mind instead of religious dogma for meaning and direction. Humanism tells us that we can deal with our own problems. We are the masters of our fate. At the heart of it all, both humanism and religion are positions of pride and stubborn self-reliance in the face of a truly impossible mission. Though the two sides may seem dia-metrically opposed, and fight each other tooth and nail in the battleground of the real world on a daily basis, they are in fact born of the same seed. This is the first response to our inescapable fate.

Atheism and Christian legalism are both born from the same impossible desire: to be the masters of our own future. Atheism says, "There is no God" in an effort to remain the highest point of authority in life. Legalism says, "Give me a list of rules that I may follow, so that at the end of the day, it is I who can take credit for the work of my own spiritual success, and pass judgment on those whom I feel have not measured up to my standards." Both ideologies are diametrically opposed to the Gospel that Jesus Christ taught that so infuriated the Pharisees of His day. Paul had some choice words for the Galatians about the Jews who were trying to convince the church there to go back under the yoke of the law:

> *I just wish that those troublemakers who want to mutilate you by circumcision would mutilate themselves. (Galatians 5:12 NLT)*

It was this desire that fouled things up to begin with. Pride went before the fall. A tree in the garden, planted to provide humanity with a choice, became its undoing. We chose to rule ourselves. We chose to disobey a loving God who had created us a pristine world to live in and offered an eternal relationship of love and community with Him. We thought we knew better; and when presented with the opportunity, we jumped at it. One tree. One choice. One Adam. Love versus selfishness. He chose wrong, and the consequence of death crashed into humanity. None would escape. Paul sums it up in Romans 3.

> *For all have sinned and fall short of the glory of God. (Romans 3:23 ESV)*

There is another response, however, one that does not

rely on our own ineffectual efforts. A divine rescue plan, set in place well before the foundations of the earth were laid, was moving right along according to schedule. This is the hope that Paul writes about in Romans 5.

> *But God shows his love for us in that while we were still sinners, Christ died for us. (Romans 5:8 ESV)*

This is the Gospel. We were hopeless. We were enemies with God. We had nothing that He needed. God didn't need our worship or love to exist. We had no bargaining chips, no leverage to use against Him. We were dead in our sin, and dead men don't have rights. He sees us in our sinful state, and He wants us as we are. It is not our job to get "cleaned up" before we come to Him. No matter what you are struggling with, no matter what you have messed up, no matter how badly you may think your past has corrupted you or how unforgivable you feel, God loves you, and He stopped at nothing to save you.

#WhatIsLove

Love is a many-splendored thing. Love is an open door. Love is a battlefield. Love is the flower you've got to let grow. Authors, poets, and wise men have written about the subject of love for millennia. Love might be defined as an intense feeling of deep affection, or "unselfish loyal and benevolent concern for the good of another."[47] Hate is not the true polar opposite of love; the true opposite of love is selfishness. In the terms of a first-grader, selfishness is when you cut in line for the swings. Love is when you let someone else take your place. Love demands action. The selfishness at the first tree in the garden was evident, but thousands of years later, there would be another garden, another tree, another choice, and another "Adam." This time the wave sweeping into the mess that man had created would be a crimson tide of cleansing sacrificial atonement. Paul writes in Romans 6:

> For the wages of sin is death, but the free gift of God is eternal life in Christ Jesus our Lord. (Romans 6:23 ESV)

The garden was Gethsemane. The second "Adam" was Jesus Christ, untainted by the line of Adam's sin. The tree was the Roman torture device that was waiting for Him if He chose to obey the Father's plan for the redemption of humanity. The choice was His. Obey and suffer, or reject and go free while condemning humanity to its deserved fate. Love versus selfishness. In the first garden, man chose wrong; but Christ would not make the same mistake. Christ alone chose love every time. He chose the cross. He chose to die in our place so a truly just

---

47. *Merriam-Webster OnLine*, s.v. "love," accessed July 19, 2017, https://www.merriam-webster.com/dictionary/love.

God could once again enter into a relationship with His fallen creation and still be pure. Through the cross sin is forgiven, but it doesn't stop there. In Christ's work on the cross, His righteousness is imputed to those who believe. Now *imputation* isn't a commonly used term these days so let's look at this a different way.

> *For our sake he made him to be sin who knew no sin, so that in him we might become the righteousness of God. (2 Corinthians 5:21 ESV)*

#TradingPlaces

One afternoon, a friend of mine opened up about a lifelong struggle he'd been battling as long as he could remember. He felt like he could never meet his father's lofty expectations for him, even though his father had long since passed. He was very mechanically gifted, but many of his cousins had graduated from Ivy League schools with high honors while he had struggled through school to graduate from a smaller local college. This perceived shortcoming plagued him well into his later years. Now, hypothetically, what if the valedictorian of Harvard University had somehow been able to legally switch transcripts with him the year of his graduation? What if all the honor and accolades heaped onto this Harvard graduate could be reassigned to his account? That, in essence, is imputation. Because of the finished work of Christ at the cross, when God looks at a person who has by faith acknowledged his or her inability to fix the problem of sin and accepted the rescue plan He has designed, He sees the righteousness of His Son. It's not just forgiveness. It's not just a fresh start. It's a perfect transcript from the Valedictorian of the universe.

Most of us crave the love and affirmation of a father figure. In our culture, it is becoming increasingly more common for that figure to come from outside the home. Wherever our father figure comes from, many of us can remember doing things in the hopes of winning his approval. When that affirmation is withheld, it can be deeply painful, and the effects can last well into adulthood. Imputation is the answer to this problem. Religion works endlessly in attempt to earn some type of eternal acceptance that a perfect and holy God could never give. The Gospel tells us that Christ has already done the work, and our acceptance by God is based solely on repentance and faith. There is no lofty list of expectations to fulfill. There is no constant comparison to others as though we are in some grand competition, as if God only has so much love to go around. These things are manmade constructs, born of pride and rooted in self-righteousness. The only righteousness that God interested in is the perfect humility of His Son, and that is what is now available to us through imputation. At the cross, Jesus allowed us, by no merit of our own, to trade our sin for His perfection.

In the first garden, at the first tree, humankind was given a choice. We chose selfishness. On the second tree, the Savior of the world made the choice to sacrifice Himself for all others. He chose love. He effectively hit the RESET button on Adam's choice for all of humanity. Through His death and resurrection, Christ had completed the crux of the divine rescue plan and opened a way for the broken relationship between God and His creation to be restored. Humanity's new choice was no longer to eat from a tree that offered a knowledge of good and evil but to accept the gift from a tree that required only one thing: repentance.

#TheHardestWordstoSay

Toddlers are adorable. My wife and I have been blessed with five, though thankfully not all at once. They are often extremely ticklish, very affectionate, passionate, authentic, and full of wonder and excitement, and their laughter is contagious. My three-year-old daughter is often the first to greet me at the door when I arrive at home, her eyes sparkling with genuine delight to see her daddy. A hug from her is a life-changing experience. She wraps her little arms around my neck, presses her cheek to mine, and squeezes with all her might. Those hugs have become one of my very favorite things. Three-year-olds seldom hold back. They have no emotional filter, no carefully maintained facade to hide behind. What you see is what you get. This works on both ends of the spectrum, however. The "terrible twos" are given that title for good reason. At that age, when children are angry, they don't play around. Selfishness is raw and exposed in all its ugliness. If they want something, they either take it or pitch a fit if they are unable to achieve their desire on their own. Toddler tantrums are a sight to behold. I don't pretend that we get any better as we get older; we simply learn to mask it more effectively. Now, my cutie-pie daughter, the same one who meets me at the door with a smile that could melt the heart of Ebenezer Scrooge, is one of the sweetest little girls I've ever been around. She is almost always so cheerful and encouraging that it's hard to believe she's only three, but every once in a while, one of her older siblings will press her buttons, and then the gloves come off. She is not to be trifled with. The claws come out, and my little angel turns into a terror, hell-bent on vengeance and fury. When the dust clears and the tears are drying, the real challenge begins: trying to get my little girl to apologize. Different kids all have different hang-ups, and this is hers. I don't know what it is, but it is mission impossible to convince her to accept responsibility for her actions, admit she was wrong, and express any level of remorse. She is not alone. Real apologies can be hard—and repentance is sometimes painful.

The message to avoid the appearance of weakness at all costs dominates our culture today, and repentance is seldom synonymous with strength in modern thought. Legally, the measures we take and resources both individuals and corporations spend to avoid any admission of guilt are staggering. No one wants to accept responsibility for their actions. No one wants to admit wrongdoing and suffer the consequences. No one dares to express any remorse. We are all overgrown three-year-olds who have become masters at masking our prideful stubbornness. It is critical that we don't confuse true repentance, which is an act of love, from abject groveling, which is hidden pride. Pride and groveling may seem like opposite extremes, but once again the truth lies in the motivation. If God freely offers forgiveness, there is no reason to try and earn favor through self-abasement. Once again, our desire to help fix our own problem trips us up, and we foolishly fall into the trap of self-reliance. We, like the couple in the first garden, at the first tree, have all chosen selfishness over love. That is why repentance is so hard. Repentance at its core is choosing love over selfishness. Repentance is the complete rejection of self-reliance. That is the choice we are now offered. God's redemption plan, made possible through the blood of His Son, hinges on that choice. God never wanted robots. He wanted beings capable of choosing to either love or reject Him.

"But you don't know what I've done..."

Some of us struggle with the idea that God could ever accept us. To truly understand the depths of the incredible forgiveness of God, we have to return to the idea of His timelessness, His *eternality* that we discussed earlier in this book. God has made it clear to us that He exists outside of time. He is I AM. That concept is one we struggle to comprehend as temporal beings, but it is critically important to the idea of divine forgiveness. When I catch myself falling back into the same old wrong patterns, it can be very discouraging. As a human, when someone else wrongs me repeatedly, it hurts anew each time. It can be hard to muster the will to forgive, but God is different than we are. When He forgives our sin at the cross, He exists at every point of failure in our lives. Nothing is new. His forgiveness is complete. There are no unpleasant surprises to Him; He knows everything we've ever done and everything we'll ever do, and His love and mercy still remain. The forgiveness of the I AM, who exists at every single point of our failure, is perfect.

#StitchinTime

Time travel has been a favorite of the sci-fi genre since its inception. From the H. G. Wells 1895 classic *The Time Machine,* to Steven Moffat's current iteration of the hit television series *Dr. Who*, to the blockbuster movie trilogy *Back to the Future*, our minds are captivated by the idea of bending the space-time continuum to our will. Should someone actually invent the technology, the possibilities would be almost infinite. What would you do with a time machine? For the sake of discussion, let's say it was a one-time use contraption, with only enough fuel for one round trip. Where would you go? What would you do? Would you become an observer to the construction of a fantas-tic architectural wonder like the Pyramids or the Great Wall, or maybe witness an incredible historic event like the Wright brothers' first flight, or the Gettysburg Address? It might be a person you'd like to meet, like Nicholi Tesla, Leonardo da Vinci, Ghengis Khan, or even Jesus Christ.

One possible answer to this question came to me recently while I was cutting down an overgrown orna-mental pear tree that had been filling my yard with rotting fruit and attracting swarms of insects. I'm not particularly handy with a chainsaw, but as it made quick work of the large nuisance, I found myself longing for a way to travel back in time to the garden of Eden with my chainsaw and simply chop down the tree. Before Adam and Eve took that fateful bite, I would cut down that blasted tree once and for all. It seemed so simple. No more temptation. No more choice. No thousands of years of suffering, pain, and war. Even if that were somehow possible, taking away the option of disobedience from the garden totally circumvents God's plan for creation. The idea that a simple, time-locked, finite human had become a better planner than the infinite, all-knowing, eternal God who created him is silly. It's easy for me to fixate on the suffering of humanity, but God's plan is so much greater.

> *For our present troubles are small and won't last very long. Yet they produce for us a glory that vastly outweighs them and will last forever! (2 Corinthians 4:17 NLT)*

God's perspective on time and history is vastly different than ours. Only He can see all outcomes, and only He knows the best way forward. We *needed* the option to choose Him. We needed the option to choose love over selfishness; but even in that choice, we needed His help. At the second tree, Christ hit the RESET button on humanity's choice to accept or reject God. Until then, we were all in the default setting of rejection. Everyone who trusted God before Jesus came was looking forward to the cross and basing their whole eternal existence on the hope of the Messiah. When Christ the Messiah came, all of that hope and faith was realized and made valid in His perfect life, sacrificial death, and resurrection. He took the sin of those who believed in Him and gave them His perfect righteousness. Paul says it in Romans 10 like this:

If you openly declare that Jesus is Lord and believe in your heart that God raised him from the dead, you will be saved. For it is by believing in your heart that you are made right with God, and it is by openly declaring your faith that you are saved. (Romans 10:9–10 NLT)

The eternal debt was paid. God was satisfied. The way gate between humanity and the divine was reopened.

. . .and everyone lived happily ever after.

Well, not exactly.

Chapter 9

#IntotheFire

We were promised sufferings. They were part of the program. We were even told, "Blessed are they that mourn," and I accept it. I've got nothing that I hadn't bargained for. Of course, it is different when the thing happens to oneself, not to others, and in reality, not imagination.

—C. S. Lewis, *A Grief Observed*

The brutality he'd witnessed was beyond measure. He had seen their handiwork with his own eyes, as refugees hobbled into his small village. Survivors were few and far between, but the ones that did manage to escape the relentless wave of soldiers were seldom without the scars to prove it. He looked up from his work long enough to see the remnants of a family, torn apart by the horrors of war, slowly wander past the courtyard in front of his house. Their hollow eyes had seen unspeakable things. A woman wrapped in a tattered shawl that held a small form walked in front, her back bent at an unnatural angle from the terrible ordeal. Behind her followed two emaciated boys struggling to keep up. The larger of the two limped along with the aid of a crude wooden crutch, his left leg gone below the knee, a common calling card of the enemy they all feared. There were no men in this group, all likely captured, killed, or worse. Jonah's eyes burned, but not with tears. It was long past time for sadness. A deep and abiding hatred filled his heart, and the rage was building inside of him. *Why is this happening? How long will my people suffer? Where is the justice?*

The Assyrians were masters of war, not just with the blade and bow, but of the mind as well. They understood how to take a city without lifting a finger. If the people of that city feared them so much that they surrendered even before the battle started, it would save valuable time and resources. Pain and brutality breed fear, so the Assyrians wielded both with masterful precision. Mass amputations, skinning people alive, great piles of severed human heads, and fields of helpless conquered foes impaled on long poles all added to the wave of dread that preceded their armies marching into battle. Jonah was all too familiar with these terrible methods of warfare as he watched the stragglers from the day's band of refugees drift in. That is why the next few moments of the life of Jonah, a prophet of God, would completely shatter his idea of who God is.

God: "Jonah."

Jonah: "Yes, God?"

God: "Get up, and go to the capital city of the Assyrians."

Jonah: "What!"

God: "I want you to go there and preach."

There are many people who condemn Jonah for running the other way, without fully understanding what God was asking him to do. He was asked to walk right into the lair of the monster. The home base of the darkest, most vile creatures he knew. The source of all of the suffering he saw all around him was now his instructed destination. Jonah, understandably, panicked. He did what many others do when presented with a situation that feels impossible. He bolted for the exit. Jonah punched his ticket on a ship going the opposite direction. He took the fastest form of transit available at the time and went the other way, and as his ship sailed out of the harbor that day, he must have felt as though an enormous weight had been lifted from his shoulders. With the briny sea breeze on his face and the sun shining down on the open water, he probably believed that he was in for smooth sailing. His problems had been solved, and he had escaped. No one could catch him now. Little did he know that his comfortable situation was about to take a turn for the worse. Like the fish in the classic fifteenth-century fable, Jonah was jumping out of the frying pan and into the fire.

#FreshStart

Therefore, if anyone is in Christ, he is a new creation. The old has passed away; behold, the new has come. (2 Corinthians 5:17 ESV)

The promise of a fresh start is the driving force behind billions of dollars of advertising in our society each year. From health clubs to nicotine patches, closet organizers to coffee, our days are constantly bombarded with products that pledge to give our lives a much-needed reset—or even just a clean start to a new day. Often, the people in these ads are smiling from ear to ear as they pedal away pounds at their local gym or laugh boisterously with their friends as they enjoy their new cigarette-free life. Carefree and contented, the hardest part of change for these people seems to have been the decision itself. Sadly, that is seldom the case. So it is with the Gospel as well. Christ had come. The rescue plan was a success. The final sacrifice was made once for all, and now redemption is freely available. God's righteous wrath against the destructive forces of sin and selfishness has been satisfied. Those who trust in the promised Messiah have been given new life in Him. The old self is gone. Everything should now be smooth sailing, right? Not exactly. Paul communicates this problem clearly three times in his letter to the Romans:

- *"I don't really understand myself, for I want to do what is right, but I don't do it. Instead, I do what I hate" (Romans 7:15 NLT).*

- *"I want to do what is good, but I don't. I don't want to do what is wrong, but I do it anyway" (Romans 7:19 NLT).*
- *"I have discovered this principle of life—that when I want to do what is right, I inevitably do what is wrong" (Romans 7:21 NLT).*

These frustrations aren't coming from just anyone struggling with their inner demons. This is the apostle Paul, leader of the early church, author of an enormous part of the New Testament, opening up about the real battle against sin in his own life, a fight that had gotten the better of him time and time again. God may have given us new life through the finished work of Christ, but nothing changed about our physical bodies. The desire to give in to sin and selfishness is still overwhelming. So here is the great question: If Paul fared so poorly against this overpowering wave of selfishness, what chance do we stand?

#LoveHurts

It had been three days with not a single word. The phone rang again and again, and with each ring the hope of reaching the intended recipient became more distant. It was so strange. My wife and I had been planning our fifteen-year anniversary trip to the islands for almost a year. It would be the first time in my life I would actually get to see crystal blue ocean water with my own eyes. As a bonus, we would be able to meet up with a few old friends I hadn't seen since college. Dano was one of them. Tall, thin, and athletic, he and I had played many hours of basketball together, and his Caribbean accent and infectious laugh were unmistakable in a crowd. Bahamian born and raised, he had a natural gift for making people feel at ease. During our time together at Bible school, I could see great potential in the way that God could use his life for the kingdom.

That hope faded as the years passed. Upon his return home, he quickly became involved with a career that took him in the opposite direction. He excelled at his new position in the entertainment industry. Our ways drifted apart until a new form of social networking was born. Through Facebook, he and I reconnected. As we became reacquainted, I kept seeing things pop up in his feed that were hard to reconcile with the person I knew from Bible college. We talked about the struggles he had been facing, and slowly, God got ahold of his heart. The change was evident. We were both really excited about the possibility of connecting on my anniversary trip, so the unanswered calls and inability to reach him was an unexpected disappointment. Finally, after three days, my cell phone rang.

It was Dano. He apologized for the delay, and we arranged a time to meet. As we sat in the hotel lobby, he began to explain the situation.

He had been in jail for three days!

I could hardly believe it. Dano explained further. He had been out of the country for several days and upon his return had been flagged, and the customs agents had pulled him from the line. Apparently, there was a warrant out for his arrest from a bank robbery ten years earlier. On the island, the system of law and order isn't always as thoroughly documented as other places. Someone else had given his name in the initial arrest report, and there were no fingerprints or even a booking photo to match. Try as he might to explain the mistake, his efforts were unsuccessful, and he was thrown in jail. The Bahamas are a tale of two realities. On one hand, the island is a posh getaway for some of the world's richest people. Magnificent yachts, luxury hotels, fine dining, and thousands of tourists with money to burn line the beaches and bays. The pristine beauty and perfect climate provide a perfect vacation spot. On the other hand, for many of the people who were born and raised Bahamian, island life is very different. Poverty is rampant. The crime rate is staggering. Many young men and women, frustrated by all the wealth that lies just out of reach, and discouraged by the lack of opportunity, turn to illicit enterprise as a way to earn fast cash. The jail Dano was now in was filled with murder suspects, most of them in their early twenties. As he lay on the hard cement slab in his cell, his mind raced. *Why did this happen to me?* At that moment, he paused his story and glanced up at me and said, "I know why this whole mess happened. During my time out of the country, I let my guard down and messed up spiritually. This was God punishing me." I looked him straight in the eye and asked, "Is that the kind of God you believe in?"

Many of us fall into that same trap. We feel like the Christian life consists of following an endless list of rules and regulations. Religion says if we don't measure up, we deserve to be punished. The Gospel says no one measures up despite our best efforts, so God sent His Son to take the consequences we deserve, and to be measured in our place so we are seen by God as perfect. The book of Jonah isn't about God punishing a wayward prophet. It isn't a cautionary tale of the perils of getting on the bad side of the divine. The book of Jonah is a love story, telling of a God of steadfast love and mercy, who is bound and determined to shape Jonah into the image of His Son, despite his incredible selfishness and stubborn disobedience. When Jonah rejected God's command to go and preach to the Ninevites, God had every right to incinerate him into a smoldering pile of ash. He could have easily found another prophet, but He didn't. God performed incredible miracles to bring Jonah's heart to the point of change. He whipped up a raging storm and then calmed it in an instant. He rigged a game of chance. He created a fish that could swallow His ornery errand boy and keep him alive for three days, not as punishment, but as a time out to think about what really mattered. This is the gift that God had given Dano: three days in a Bahamian prison with no cell phone, no e-mail, and no distractions—time to simply think about his life. It was the gift of perspective.

Jonah was so blinded by hatred and selfishness that he had lost perspective on the things that were truly important. Don't be quick to judge him. Nineveh was the capital of the Assyrian Empire, and as we discussed earlier, the Assyrian Empire was one of the most brutal and horrific perpetrators of cruelty in warfare to date. Still, God loved them and wanted to see them repent, just as He wanted His prophet to see the ugliness in his own heart and repent. Jonah did repent, and God performed another miracle and commanded the fish to spit him out onto dry land. Jonah must have been a real sight to see. Three days stewing in the stomach acid of a sea creature can't be good for one's complexion. Jonah preached in Nineveh, and the whole city threw itself on the mercy of God. Once again, Jonah's selfishness overcame him, and instead of rejoicing at the thousands who have found grace, he was angry. He felt like justice had been cheated, and that the Ninevites should not have received mercy. Conveniently, he ignored the last few extensions of grace in his own life. God then miraculously caused a shady plant to grow over his sulking servant, providing his burning skin a much-needed respite from the hot Mediterranean sun. Peeling back the layers of Jonah's heart, God then used a simple worm to expose the selfish nature that lay hidden there. The worm killed the plant, and when an angry Jonah complained to God, his sin was laid bare.

> *Then the LORD said, "You feel sorry about the plant, though you did nothing to put it there. It came quickly and died quickly. But Nineveh has more than 120,000 people living in spiritual darkness, not to mention all the animals. Shouldn't I feel sorry for such a great city?" (Jonah 4:10–11 NLT)*

Ouch. What a reality check. Jonah is a perfect example of the sanctification process. The whole book can be perfectly summed up in one verse from Paul to the church in Philippi.

> *And I am certain that God, who began the good work within you, will continue his work until it is finally finished on the day when Christ Jesus returns. (Philippians 1:6 NLT)*

This is spiritual life after the rescue plan. This is

how spiritual growth works. It is not a checklist of self-improvement as prescribed by every other world religion. Just like the rescue plan for humanity, God's design for our growth process is "by grace through faith."

#ThePerfectDay

Look at it this way: suppose I get up in the morning and have the perfect day. I don't yell at my kids or kick my dog, and I treat my wife with respect and love. I don't bad-mouth my boss at work or surf the Internet looking for porn. In every problem, I am patient and kind to others. At the end of the day, who gets the credit for that? I lay my head on my pillow and think, *Wow. What a great day. I am so disciplined. I worked hard.* This way of thinking also leads to the pitfall of comparing others to the items on your list and sitting in judgment of them when they don't measure up. That is the gospel of self. It is the idea that we can make our own way. On the other hand, if I get up and say, "God, I'm completely lost without You. I need You today just as desperately as I needed You the moment You brought me from death to life. I can do nothing without You. Grow me closer to You, and make me more like Your Son. If You don't do this in me, it's not going to happen." That's not just a formulaic prayer first thing in the morning. It is an open conversation, full of dependence on and submission to a God who is intimately involved with His children. Then if I have a great day, who gets the credit for that? When I lay my head down at night, I can celebrate the God who continues His work in me. That is the Gospel. It is by His grace through our faith.

There is a passage in the last book of the Bible that talks about the future, when all of those who have been murdered for their faith in Christ are given crowns of glory. They have been through terrible things. If anyone ever deserved a trophy, this would be the time, and yet we find them laying their crowns back at the feet of their Savior. It simply doesn't make sense in the construct of a meritocracy, but in the light of the Gospel, it's the only logical thing to do. I can just imagine one of these martyrs, standing on the floor of the great Roman Coliseum, surrounded by jeering crowds crying out for blood as the lions strain against their bonds waiting to be released, drops to her knees in prayer. *God, I cannot face this trial alone. I do not have the strength or courage to withstand this ordeal. You are my Rock, my Hiding Place, my ever-present help in times of trouble. I submit to You. If You don't do this in me, I will fail.* In seconds the beasts devour the helpless victims, yet they are able to stand unflinching. As they step into eternity and are greeted by the One who came to rescue them from eternal death, it only makes sense that any reward they are given would immediately be redirected to the One who worked in them, giving them strength and courage to accomplish the work He had started. They saw reality. Their perspective was crystal clear. This is sanctification. It is not dutifully following a list of rules. It is not a Herculean feat of self-discipline. It is not a checklist of spiritual merit badges. It is complete and total dependence on the One who is working in us until the day of His return. There is no room for prideful arrogance in the Gospel. Our growth is not a result of our own ability and work. It is Christ, through the Holy Spirit, working in us.

While getting my hair cut a few days ago, I asked the stylist to name the first adjective that came to his mind when I said the word *Christian*. Unsurprisingly, he responded, "Judgmental." Checklist Christianity leads to this critical, condemning spirit toward others. If we are basing our self-worth on our ability to follow a set of rules, we are always going to fail, and in that failure, we try and make ourselves feel better by looking for others who are failing in ways we deem worse than our own. We are in bondage to the law that was meant to expose our universal need for a Savior. The struggle with sin is real. It is foolish to think that I might be able to be victorious in that struggle on my own now, when almost two thousand years ago the man who wrote a huge part of the New Testament, a leader in the early church, and a faithful martyr for his belief, penned the words, "I do what I don't want to do and I don't want to do what I do" and "Who will save me from this body of death?" If Paul couldn't handle it, I sure can't. So what is the solution?

#Interference

Both of my boys love radio control cars. For Christmas one year, we got them each similar cars to play with. On each box was a small but very important number followed with the letters "mhz." This is the frequency at which the controller communicates with the car. It is of utmost importance that these numbers not be the same if you should buy two for your kids to use together, as we quickly learned. The results were chaotic. Two frustrated boys wondered why their cars were zipping around wildly and smashing into any object unlucky enough to be caught in their path as they tried in vain to steer their new vehicles. I couldn't help but dread the future stage of teaching them to drive as I watched the confusion unfold. Eventually, we figured out that their controllers were interfering with one another. Two people attempting to control the same car does not work. This is similar to the frustration we feel as we try to walk in the way Christ has modeled for us. The tainted, sinful body that we received at birth does not disappear on the day we accept the gift of life that Jesus made possible when He completed the rescue plan. We know what is right, but the struggle for control against our flesh is real and exhausting.

> *For those who live according to the flesh set their minds on the things of the flesh, but those who live according to the Spirit set their minds on the things of the Spirit. For to set the mind on the flesh is death, but to set the mind on the Spirit is life and peace. (Romans 8:5–6 ESV)*

The struggle is real. Within each of us there are two forces locked in perpetual combat for control. In the end, we are left with unmet expectations and a load of guilt for failure from mistakes and lapses in judgment, scars from the fight with our flesh. It is overwhelming, but Romans 8 opens with hope and a critical reminder.

> *So now there is no condemnation for those who belong to Christ Jesus. And because you belong to him, the power of the life-giving Spirit has freed you from the power of sin that leads to death. (Romans 8:1–2 NLT)*

No condemnation. Freedom from guilt. The chains of self-loathing are shattered. The checklist, do-it-yourself way of sanctification is obsolete. If Jesus bought into that ideal, the Pharisees would have been his closest friends. They never missed church. They gave to the poor. They prayed openly. They memorized the Scripture like no one else, but Christ hammered them with some of His harshest recorded words. Why? It all comes back to motivation, selfishness, and love. What they were doing was motivated by selfishness. Jesus could see into their hearts, and the sin that consumed them up like cancer was revealed. We are free from the power of sin by the power of the "life-giving Spirit." What is this strange force? How does it work?

#ExactlyWhatWeNeeded

God is a relational God. Since humanity is made in His Image, we too are relational beings. The need for community is one of the most fundamental dependencies of the human condition. There are few things more crushing than the feeling that you are completely and utterly alone. I'm not talking about voluntary solitude but the kind of extreme loneliness and seclusion that tears at the fabric of the mind. Supreme Court Justice Anthony Kennedy noted in a decision in the case of Hector Ayala, a convicted prisoner who has been on California's death row for twenty-five years and solitary confinement for most of that, this sort of "near-total isolation exacts a terrible price."[48] The desire to belong is so compelling that

---

48. Editorial board, "Justice Kennedy on Solitary Confinement," *New York Times*, June 19, 2015, http://www.nytimes.com/2015/06/20/opinion/justice-kennedy-on-solitary-confinement.html.

most of our lives are spent in pursuit of that aim. The more that we try to fix our situation, the worse things become. The emptiness in our hearts can never really be filled by other imperfect people. We are desperately in need of relationship, not only with each other, but with the God who formed and fashioned us and sent His Son to rescue us from our separation from Him. We cannot hope to live the life that God has designed for us without Him doing it in us. Jesus gives us hope in a discussion with His disciples in John 14.

> *"I will not leave you as orphans; I will come to you. Yet a little while and the world will see me no more, but you will see me. Because I live, you also will live. In that day you will know that I am in my Father, and you in me, and I in you." (John 14:18–20 ESV)*

> *"These things I have spoken to you while I am still with you. But the Helper, the Holy Spirit, whom the Father will send in my name, he will teach you all things and bring to your remembrance all that I have said to you. Peace I leave with you; my peace I give to you. Not as the world gives do I give to you. Let not your hearts be troubled, neither let them be afraid." (John 14:25–27 ESV)*

The Holy Spirit is the indwelling presence of the third person of the Trinity that we receive when we repent and believe in the Gospel, God's rescue plan for humanity, and in Christ Jesus, the second person in the Trinity, who has come to pay the penalty of sin for all who believe. The Spirit will never leave us, and in Him we have everything we need. In Him, we find peace and refuge.

An invisible spirit, with no way to be measured or quantified, sounds a lot like the imaginary friend of a small child. What separates the experience of a creative little one from the one Jesus describes in John 14? Of all the evidences of the reality of the presence of the Holy Spirit in our lives, the one that is often overlooked is one of the most powerful: the conviction of sin. I love the story that Matt Chandler, a pastor in Texas, tells about his son. After a late night, the father came out to the living room to find him playing a game on his Xbox.

> *I just walked in and did my fatherly duty. I said, "Hey, bro. Is your room clean?"*
>
> *He sighed.*
>
> *"Did you just breathe out on me, bro?"*
>
> *"No, I was just breathing."*
>
> *He paused to go and clean his room. Then his other chore is to vacuum the house. I go to start unloading the dishwasher and making our bed. I heard the vacuum go for about forty-five seconds. Then Reid was like, "I'm done."*
>
> *I was like, "You vacuumed the whole house?"*
>
> *"Uh-huh."*

"Son, Superman could not vacuum this whole house in forty-five seconds."

"I did, Dad."

I did what a loving father would do. I grabbed his hand. I said, "Let's just walk around and see." We just walked around the house, and over in this corner, we found what looked to be that one of my children opened up one of those bags of Goldfish and then dumped it and then danced on it, so I asked Reid, "Did you vacuum this?"

"I didn't see it."

"Okay, but it's on the floor. You're supposed to vacuum the floor. I don't know how you missed this."

We vacuumed. We walked around, and I would show him.

The reason I love this little sentence, "We will make our house with him," is because what is being illustrated is not that our whole house is clean but that our love and desire for our house to be clean has invited in the power of the Holy Spirit and the presence of God so they walk our house with us and go, "Hey, look at these crushed up Goldfish. It's going to be awesome for them to be gone. Bugs are going to get in here, and bad stuff is going to happen. There's going to be a smell in here. Let's get this cleaned up. I'm going to help *you get that cleaned up."*

This story is a picture of the incredible role of the Spirit that Jesus is speaking of in John 14:23:

"If anyone loves me, he will keep my word, and my Father will love him, and we will come to him and make our home with him." (ESV)

He comes to make a home in us. He walks with us through the home of our hearts to point out and help clean up the garbage that has been festering there that we may have "missed." In our hearts, God continues to open areas and clean up spaces that we never even realized were problematic.[49]

Let me be clear: there is a distinct difference between the Holy Spirit's convicting work and human performance-based feelings of crushing guilt. The latter is a result of our own striving for approval through accomplishment. As we have examined, that is the same system as every other world religion. Conviction from the Holy Spirit is a call to repentance and submission. It spurs action and change, all the while reminding us that we are incapable of changing ourselves. True life change comes when we acknowledge our own inadequacies and fall on our faces at the foot of the cross, where Christ in us takes control. This is not a "once and done" commitment; it is a

---

49. Matt Chandler, "I Believe in the Holy Spirit" (sermon), October 25, 2015. Used with permission.

lifelong daily conversation of trusting the God who began a good work in you to be faithful to complete it. This is not a humanistic guilt complex. It is a loving God/Holy Spirit at work. He whispers to us when we are confronted with temptation and in danger of wrecking our lives on the rocks of poor decisions, and comforts us in the wake of heartache and tragedy. He gently reminds us that the things we think we want so badly are empty and hollow compared to the joy that is offered in the design for life lived according to His commands. C. S. Lewis says it masterfully in his book of talks *The Weight of Glory*.

> *If we consider the unblushing promises of reward and the staggering nature of the rewards promised in the Gospels, it would seem that Our Lord finds our desires not too strong, but too weak. We are half-hearted creatures, fooling about with drink and sex and ambition when infinite joy is offered us, like an ignorant child who wants to go on making mud pies in a slum because he cannot imagine what is meant by the offer of a holiday at the sea. We are far too easily pleased.[50]*

The Holy Spirit reminds us of this truth. It recalibrates our perspectives to the eternal. It speaks through the Scripture in Romans 8.

---

50. C. S. Lewis, "The Weight of Glory" in *The Weight of Glory and Other Addresses*, ed. W. Hooper (New York: Simon and Schuster, 1996), 25–26.

Yet what we suffer now is nothing compared to the glory he will reveal to us later. For all creation is waiting eagerly for that future day when God will reveal who his children really are. Against its will, all creation was subjected to God's curse. But with eager hope, the creation looks forward to the day when it will join God's children in glorious freedom from death and decay. For we know that all creation has been groaning as in the pains of childbirth right up to the present time. And we believers also groan, even though we have the Holy Spirit within us as a foretaste of future glory, for we long for our bodies to be released from sin and suffering. We, too, wait with eager hope for the day when God will give us our full rights as his adopted children, including the new bodies he has promised us. We were given this hope when we were saved. (If we already have something, we don't need to hope for it. But if we look forward to something we don't yet have, we must wait patiently and confidently.) (Romans 8:18–25 NLT)

This new perspective is critical to understanding who we are in Christ. When we have an accurate view of ourselves, and an accurate perspective of our Savior, our absolute dependence is exposed. Troubles will come. Problems will pile up into mountains of stress and pain. Sometimes the levels of frustration or grief we are forced to deal with are so overwhelming that we don't even know what to pray about, but even then our Comforter lovingly cares for us.

And the Holy Spirit helps us in our weakness. For example, we don't know what God wants us to pray for. But the Holy Spirit prays for us with groanings that cannot be expressed in words. And the Father who knows all hearts knows what the Spirit is saying, for the Spirit pleads for us believers in harmony with God's own will. (Romans 8:26–27 NLT)

There are few things more assuring in a crisis situation than the knowledge that someone very powerful is on your side. In our weakness, He is made strong. When we don't have the words, the Holy Spirit does, and His words are perfectly in sync with the will of the Father. He is not a God just waiting for the opportunity to throw us in jail for three days when we sin. His love is not performance based. He knows our hearts and cares for us deeply. This leads us to one of the most overquoted and misrepresented verses in the whole Bible.

And we know that God causes everything to work together for the good of those who love God and are called according to his purpose for them. (Romans 8:28 NLT)

He is working all things out for our good. Everything will work out in the end. Many use this to justify their pursuit of happiness, or as evidence that God will remove pain from our lives. This couldn't be further from the truth. Hebrews 11, the famous "hall of faith" chapter, is filled with people whose lives ended in horrific ways for the cause of Christ. Did they not love God? One of the things that really frustrates me is when people attempt to console a person grappling with extreme hardship and pain by explaining just how they think God is working in the situation. "Your daughter has run away so that you can understand better what it means to have grace and mercy." "Your cancer has come back to teach you to trust in His wisdom." "Your child died so that others could know God and accept His Gospel." Just stop. This trivializes the pain of others. I'm not saying that God's plan is completely unknowable, but to try and distill the countless machinations of the Infinite mind into a simple reason a finite human brain could grasp is sheer lunacy. Our "good" is not necessarily being cured from cancer. Our good might not be landing the new job we feel we desperately need. Our good may not be pain free—indeed, if the disciples are any indication, it probably won't be. Eternal perspective is needed. In ten thousand years, we will see the back of the tapestry, where all the pain and strife of earth are woven into a beautiful masterpiece of grace, mercy, and love. For now, we trust Him, knowing that He is in control and working things together for good. His love is not based on our performance; for even in our weakness, His goodness shines through.

> *And I am convinced that nothing can ever separate us from God's love. Neither death nor life, neither angels nor demons, neither our fears for today nor our worries about tomorrow—not even the powers of hell can separate us from God's love. No power in the sky above or in the earth below—indeed, nothing in all creation will ever be able to separate us from the love of God that is revealed in Christ Jesus our Lord. (Romans 8:38–39 NLT)*

The whole story of God's rescue plan is a juggernaut of love, mercy, and kindness blazing down through history to rescue humanity from the consequences of their own actions, and restore the relationship broken by sin. What God has joined together, let no one separate. We usually hear those words in a marriage ceremony, but in our society, half of all marriages end in divorce. Human love is a fickle thing, and selfishness runs rampant, but our restoration to God is unbreakable. Love is not just something God does; it is who He is. When God makes a promise, He keeps it, and His promise to grow us into the likeness of His Son is unconditional. This brings us back to Philippians 1:6: He will be faithful to complete His work in us. There is no conditional terminology there. Does it read, "He will be faithful if you follow your checklist"? How about, "He will be faithful as long as you don't screw up too badly"? No. *Nothing* can separate us from His love. He will not be stopped. It is not your job to make yourself like Christ on your own. Trust God. Abide in Him. Saturate yourself with His Word. Delve deeply into a community of like-minded believers, not for spiritual bonus points or gold star stickers on a Sunday school achievement chart, but because you see your own weakness and genuine dependence on His perfect strength.

#FishFried

The equatorial heat was oppressive, and on the tender flesh that had spent three days in the digestive tract of a huge fish, it was brutally intensified. Jonah glowered and grimaced in pain as he readjusted his position, hunkering down in the small shelter he had built for himself east of the city. At least this leafy green plant that had grown up into the ramshackle hovel provided some relief from the harsh rays of the sun. How could God forgive a city whose wealth and prestige was built on mountains of dismembered corpses? How could God let a people who thrived on the suffering of others go unpunished? They did not deserve mercy. Jonah spit in the direction of Nineveh as his anger seethed within him. *Unbelievable.* The fury he felt was exhausting, and he soon fell asleep, a sweet release from the misery that was now his constant companion. The respite was short lived, however, and he awoke to the searing pain of the burning sun on his raw skin. The plant that had provided precious shade just hours before had withered into a dry husk. Upon closer inspection, Jonah saw that a tiny worm had eaten into the core stalk, cutting off its nutrient supply and effectively dooming it to the hot, arid climate.

> *And as the sun grew hot, God arranged for a scorching east wind to blow on Jonah. The sun beat down on his head until he grew faint and wished to die. "Death is certainly better than living like this!" he exclaimed.*
> *Then God said to Jonah, "Is it right for you to be angry because the plant died?"*
> *"Yes," Jonah retorted, "even angry enough to die!"*
> *Then the LORD said, "You feel sorry about the plant, though you did nothing to put it there. It came quickly and died quickly. But Nineveh has more than 120,000 people living in spiritual darkness, not to mention all the animals. Shouldn't I feel sorry for such a great city?" (Jonah 4:8–11 NLT)*

Perspective. It was the thing Jonah lacked that he desperately needed more than any other. God hadn't given up on His ornery, defiant messenger. He loved him so much that He would continue to do His work in Jonah. His love was unstoppable, for Jonah and the city nearby that now celebrated in the mercy and grace of their newfound God. Whether you find perspective in the joy of new birth or the misery of a three-night stay in a lonely prison cell, God never gives up on those who have accepted the truth of His Gospel, and it is that perspective that He uses to push us onward, even through the inferno of trials of life here on earth.

If our new lives in Christ are truly "out of the frying pan, into the fire," it is reassuring to know that we serve a risen Savior who is no stranger to the flames. There are three Hebrew boys who can attest to that, and if He is with us in the fire, there can be no better place.[51]

---

51. Daniel 3

Chapter 10
#MidnightRescue

When we have been brought very low and helped, sorely wounded and healed, cast down and raised again, have given up all hope—and been suddenly snatched from danger, and placed in safety; and when these things have been repeated to us and in us a thousand times over, we begin to learn to trust simply to the word and power of God, beyond and against appearances.

—JOHN NEWTON

The ocean tore at the darkened coastline with all the fury of a raging nor'easter. The cold February winds had whipped the sea into swells that reached sixty feet high, and the storm had not abated during the night. Thirty-three men now huddled on the deck of a broken tanker ship, ripped in two by the tempest that surrounded them. Their chance of rescue was bleak. Between their wrecked vessel and the safety of the shoreline loomed the Chatham bar, a grouping of rocky shoals that was treacherous even on the best of days, but suicidal to attempt crossing on this stormy night. The tanker *Pendleton* had broken apart with no warning, just the sudden deafening roar of steel tearing and cracking, weakened by shoddy production. They had been unable to send a distress call and were now at the mercy of the sea. Forty-one men had set out on the tanker's voyage from New Orleans to Boston. Eight had been caught on the bow when it had cracked and filled with seawater, lost to the depths of the unforgiving ocean. The remaining sailors peered through the darkness and driving snow, vainly straining for any glimmer of hope. Suddenly, one of them cried out, his arm pointing to a small gleam tossing about in the punishing sea.

Bernard "Bernie" Webber was a petty officer assigned to the US Coast Guard at Station Chatham, Massachusetts. Born and raised on the coast of Massachusetts, he was well aware of the dangers a strong nor'easter could bring to a ship in distress. Earlier that night, a call came in about a ship sighted in distress beyond the bar. Any attempt at rescue was nigh suicidal, so when given the order by their commanding officer to attempt to reach the sinking tanker, most of the men in the station had either refused or disappeared, and no one could blame them. Only three remained, Richard Livesey, Andrew Fitzgerald, and Ervin Maske. Understanding the almost-certain fate that lay ahead, the four men headed out into the storm in a thirty-six-foot CG-36500 Motor Lifeboat. Designed to operate in extreme conditions, the self-righting boat was still outmatched by the colossal waves, at times higher than a five-story building, as it struggled through the darkness. The rocky shoals ahead lay in wait, ready to smash the small vessel to pieces. Carefully, Webber and his crew guided the boat through the storm, admittedly terrified by the peril of the night. Timing the engine with the breakers, they barely made the crossing of the bar, only to have a giant wave lift their ten-ton craft out of the water and send it airborne, crashing down onto its side, shattering the windshield and tearing their only working compass from its mounting. The sturdy little lifeboat righted itself and motored on, with only a searchlight to help them locate the *Pendleton* in the darkness. The sound of twisting metal alerted them to the broken tanker ship's location. The gigantic waves would roll the boat so far over that the single ninety-horsepower gasoline engine would die out due to fuel starvation. Engineer Andy Fitzgerald would then have to crawl into the cramped engine compartment to restart it, leaving him with severe burns and bruises.[52] Finally, after what seemed like an eternity, the roving light from the CG-36500 caught a glimpse of the badly

---

52. "The Finest Hours," *History vs. Hollywood*, accessed July 19, 2017, http://www.historyvshollywood.com/reelfaces/finest-hours/.

listing tanker. The daring rescue of the thirty-three men trapped on the *Pendleton* was about to begin.[53, 54, 55, 56]

#Teambuilding

What kind of people risk their lives for people they've never even met? Were the ones who stayed behind in safety wrong for valuing their own lives more? At what point is fear a compelling reason to avoid risk?

In the divine rescue plan, it's important to define our roles. In Romans 9, Paul transitions from the newfound life available to us through the Gospel to our part in the plan to rescue others.

> *But how can they call on him to save them unless they believe in him? And how can they believe in him if they have never heard about him? And how can they hear about him unless someone tells them? And how will anyone go and tell them without being sent? That is why the Scriptures say, "How beautiful are the feet of messengers who bring good*

53. Eliza Berman, "The True Story Behind *The Finest Hours*," *Time*, January 29, 2016, http://time.com/4197131/the-finest-hours-true-story/.

54. *Wikipedia*, s.v. "SS Pendleton," last modified July 13, 2017, https://en.wikipedia.org/wiki/SS_Pendleton.

55. *Wikipedia*, s.v. "*The Finest Hours (2016 film)*," last modified July 10, 2017, https://en.wikipedia.org/wiki/The_Finest_Hours_(2016_film).

56. Michael J. Tougias and Casey Sherman, *The Finest Hours: The True Story of the U.S. Coast Guard's Most Daring Sea Rescue* (New York: Scribner, 2009).

news!" (Romans 10:14–15 NLT)

We are the messengers. We get to be a part of the great rescue ourselves. God in His infinite wisdom has allowed us to be a part of the rescue team!

#PawPatrol

Sirens blare and lights blaze. Engines roar to life, and theme music echoes out over the pandemonium. "Go, go, go, go!" is chanted over and over as small dogs tumble down a large slide, spiraling out of their tower command center into their awaiting rescue vehicles. Each member of the team is different. From a pink-uniformed cocker spaniel that flies a small helicopter to a clumsy Dalmatian medic in a fire truck, these dogs are on a mission, to rescue some hapless victim from impending doom. Welcome to *Paw Patrol*, one of my three-year-old daughter's favorite TV shows. As a father of five, I have seen my share of children's television shows, and so many of them now revolve around this idea of a rescue squad. From Lassie rescuing Timmy from the well to cartoon canines driving rescue vehicles into the brink of disaster, the idea of helping someone in dire need is a consistent theme. We all long to be part of something bigger, something that matters. If we are to be good team members, there are two things that we need to be very clear on: the ability to see who needs rescuing, and the plan for how to go about it.

#ControlIssues

I lay motionless in the blackness, wondering if I'd just made one of the biggest mistakes of my life. It felt as though my eyes had been assaulted by a sand blaster. Any light that penetrated my firmly shut eyelids burned like fire. The world changes greatly when you lose the ability to see. An ability you depend on every day can be taken for granted so easily. Normally my eyesight is bad—bad enough, in fact, to be classified as legally blind without glasses or contacts. Now I couldn't even open my eyes to see my hand in front of my face. The easiest tasks became impossible, and simply walking from one room to another was now a perilous adventure without the help of someone to guide me. The surgeon had said these things could be expected, but experiencing them was something else entirely. It was frustrating before to wake up in the middle of the night and fumble around for my glasses on the nightstand, but now there were no glasses to remedy my problem. All I could do was wait.

Humans often overestimate our abilities. We think we see things around us fairly well. In a way, we are correct. Vision correction is more advanced and effective than any other time in history. We have microscopes to see down to the atomic level. In 2015, Lawrence Berkeley National Labs turned on a $27 million electron microscope with the capability to make images to a resolution of half the width of a hydrogen atom. We have telescopes powerful enough to see galaxies that are vast distances from our own. With the invention of video recording, we can watch current events take place thousands of miles from us and observe incidents like the Kennedy assassination that took place almost fifty years ago. Even with all this technology, however, our field of vision is incredibly limited. I can't see ten inches behind my own head without the help of a mirror, let alone the deer in the road around the next bend as I drive. Everything we can actually see is limited to the instant in which we exist, and depending on position and visibility, a few miles around on a clear day. The things we cannot see far outnumber the things we can. We are consumed with the pursuit of technology that will allow us to see further and look closer than ever before. We have an overwhelming thirst for knowledge in the spiritual realms as well. Humans have studied for entire lifetimes in an attempt to begin to understand the Infinite. Theologians and scholars have devoted their time and energy to write great volumes on the makeup of God and His divine nature. This is all well and good. God has revealed Himself to us through His Word and wants us to know Him. The problem arises when we ascribe characteristics to Him that are not expressly divulged in His Word. Let's go back to the idea of pouring an infinite ocean into a coffee mug that we discussed earlier. If the knowledge of God is truly endless, and our minds have a finite capacity to learn, when the former is poured into the latter, its capacity can only contain a tiny fraction of the flood of infinite knowledge.

Over the millennia, many extrapolations have been offered up as truth, some of which even find their roots in biblical fact. Entire theological divisions have arisen and caused massive conflict between those who bear the name of Christ followers, even to the point of all-out war. In the early seventeenth century, a great schism in the church occurred over one of the questions that we are discussing in this chapter: "Who exactly needs rescuing, and whose job is it?" Hold on tight, because we are about to do a cannonball into the deep end of the pool of theology.

Romans 9 can be one of the most difficult passages in the whole Bible.

> *So you see, God chooses to show mercy to some, and he chooses to harden the hearts of others so they refuse to listen. (Romans 9:18 NLT)*

Verses like that tell us that God is the one who determines who is rescued, and who is not. John Calvin, an influential French theologian and pastor during the

Protestant Reformation, was a strong proponent of this idea. His thoughts have been collected into a movement called Calvinism. Calvinists believe that sin so affects human nature that we are unable even to exercise faith in Christ by our own will. God has chosen from eternity those whom He will draw to Himself.

This all seems to make sense until we read verses in Romans 10 like these:

> *As the Scriptures tell us, "Anyone who trusts in him will never be disgraced." Jew and Gentile are the same in this respect. They have the same Lord, who gives generously to all who call on him. For "Everyone who calls on the name of the Lord will be saved." (Romans 10:11–13 NLT)*

This passage, just a few short verses from the first, clearly says that we have the ability to choose to be rescued or not. It says that *everyone* who desires salvation will be saved. This seems to be diametrically opposed to the idea that God determines redemption. Jacobus Arminius, a Dutch pastor and theologian in the late sixteenth and early seventeenth centuries, took this position, founding the school of thought named for him—Arminianism. Arminianists highlight the free will of humanity, our ability to choose the redemption provided by Christ's sacrifice.

So, which is it? Are we all predestined by God for glory

or judgment? Are we free to choose our own path? How does the eternal "I AM" who exists unbound by time and space *pre- anything*? Remember what happened when we talked about pouring the infinite into a finite container? This is the part where the idea of infinite spillage is key.

In our quest to know God, we have a habit of bending truths that we don't quite understand to better fit our carefully constructed theological frameworks. This is incredibly dangerous. Knowledge is power, and we are so desperate for God to fit in the ideological boxes that we have built that we ignore or deny the parts of His existence that don't match our concept of Him. We have built God in our own image, and the end product is really no god at all. Trading the truth for a lie, as Paul speaks of in Romans 1, makes us all fools. Our desire to completely understand and contain the infinite leads us down a dark path. We need to be willing to say, "I don't know" sometimes and base our faith on the revealed Word He has given us. Does God determine who is rescued? Yes. Do humans have the ability to choose eternal life or death based on the finished work of Christ? Yes. How do those two seemingly contradictory statements coexist? I don't know. It may have something to do with God not being confined to time like we are. Who knows? All we can know is that He has revealed both concepts to be true according to Scripture, and it is not my job to explain every divine mystery. One day all will be clear. Just as my eyes have now healed from surgery, and my vision is now sharper than it has ever been, there will come a day when we are together with our Creator and all things will come into focus. There may be pain in the process, but the pain will be well worth it when we finally see our Savior face-to-face.

#BeautifulFeet

As the men on Bernie Webber's life boat wrestled with the raging sea in their life-or-death battle for the lives of the stranded crew of the crippled *Pendleton*, they, too, needed razor-sharp clarity on what their goal and plan of action was. There was no room for error, no time for second guessing. Their very lives depended on their mission.

The lifeboat pitched and rolled in the angry waves, each one seemingly more brutal than the last. With the damaged ship finally in sight, it was a miracle that they had made it this far. Before Webber had made the choice to leave the mainland, he'd understood the difficulty and risk involved with this rescue operation. The men at the Coast Guard station did as well, as evidenced by the sudden disappearance of so many of them. Webber understood that he could not hope to run this mission alone. He needed a team he could trust, dependable men who were able to fill their respective roles well while unflinchingly staring death in the face. Superheroes are for comic books. A well-oiled team is far superior in real life. In Romans 10, Paul makes an impassioned call for others to join the divine rescue team:

> For "Everyone who calls on the name of the LORD will be saved." But how can they call on him to save them unless they believe in him? And how can they believe in him if they have never heard about him? And how can they hear about him unless someone tells them? And how will anyone go and tell them without being sent? That is why the Scriptures say, "How beautiful are the feet of messengers who bring good news!" (Romans 10:13–15 NLT)

This is not a selective request for an elite, seminary-trained evangelistic task force. This is an "All hands on deck!" appeal for help from every person who has been rescued from the kingdom of darkness into the kingdom of marvelous light. If you have experienced the forgiveness of the Father through the work of the Son, this means you!

Many of us have the same reaction to God's rallying cry for rescue team members that Moses had at the burning bush.

> But God, I'm not qualified.
> I can't speak well.

I'm too scared to talk to others about this stuff.
I don't know what to say.

Our objections today are just as absurd as Moses' were in light of the infinite God that we serve. It has never been our job to convince others to accept the truth of the Gospel. We are simply the messengers bearing the good news. God Himself accomplishes salvation. So how then do we get started? What is the best way to get "beautiful feet"?

#ThePowerofaStory

The sounds of shuffling feet on the dusty road and the muffled din of busy townspeople milling about the marketplace were sounds he knew well. After years of begging in this very spot, the place had slowly become his home. He could tell the creaking wagon of the tent vendor from the rhythmic clacking of iron-rimmed wheels of the pottery cart, filled with cooking pots, decorative jars, and clay bowls for sale. The pungent scent of the fishmonger washing away the remnants of today's catch from his stand permeated the air. The man lifted his head as he heard a strange but calming voice. He saw nothing. He had seen nothing since the day of his birth. The blind beggar cupped a hand to his ear and craned his neck forward. The voice came from a man, a teacher, walking nearby with his followers.

"Rabbi," his disciples asked him, "why was this man born blind? Was it because of his own sins or his parents' sins?"

"It was not because of his sins or his parents' sins," Jesus answered. "This happened so the power of God could be seen in him." (John 9:2–3 NLT)

Jesus stopped in front of him. He reached down and smeared something warm over his eyes. Suddenly the world flashed into view in a kaleidoscope of brilliant light. For the first time in his entire life, he could see! Quickly word spread all over town, and the religious leaders of the day flew into a rage. They *hated* Jesus. He eroded the power they held through suffocating religious law, and he was a threat. The leaders dragged the once-blind man before the council and peppered him with questions. His answer was simple and concise.

"I was blind, and now I can see!" (John 9:25 NLT)

Shockwaves rippled through the courtroom. The man was not a trained orator with a special gift of public speaking and superhuman persuasive powers. He simply told his story, and God used it in a powerful way.

Another time, Jesus was passing through a town of Samaria, home to a people group traditionally maligned and discriminated against by the Jewish community of the day. He stopped to talk with a Samaritan woman drawing water at the village well. She was no pillar of her community. Her many failed marriages and current status as a live-in girlfriend were repulsive to the culture of her day, and she was probably drawing water in the relentless heat of midday to avoid as many people as possible. High noon in a Mediterranean climate is not an ideal time for hauling large, heavy containers of water. Jesus calmly struck up a conversation with the woman that "dignified" people of the day wouldn't dare to so much as acknowledge. He cut through the facade and touched her heart with His love and compassionate truth. She was so moved that she brought the whole town to hear the man who told her the incredible good news of redemption. She was no person of influence, no celebrity, no popularity contest winner, but when the people in her town heard her story, they were compelled to come and see for themselves. This is the way the Gospel works. Everyone can tell their own story of repentance, submission, and dependence. It is not our job to convince people that the Gospel is true. We are not all required to be academic apologists or world champion debaters. God is the One who changes hearts; we are simply the messengers. This is how the beautiful feet Paul talks about in Romans 10 are made! We are all called to be the "Good News bringers." We are all called to be part of the rescue team.

Fear and anxiety are normal feelings when we are given the opportunity to share what Christ has done in our lives, but it is in the center of that fear that He comes to us, just as He walked across the waters to the terrified fishermen. He assures us that He is with us and calls us to obey and follow Him. With a word, He can calm our hearts, from tempest to stillness, from fury to absolute calm, the storm over. We, like Peter, can lose perspective. We forget that the Maker of the storm was the One who has called us and allow the fear of the situation to supersede the glory and power of our Creator. What an incredible Savior! At the end of Romans 11, Paul wraps up this section by anchoring our role in the rescue plan to Him.

> *Oh, how great are God's riches and wisdom and knowledge! How impossible it is for us to understand his decisions and his ways! For who can know the LORD's thoughts? Who knows enough to give him advice? And who has given him so much that he needs to pay it back? For everything comes from him and exists by his power and is intended for his glory. All glory to him forever! Amen. (Romans 11:33–36 NLT)*

Sharing your story can be scary. Vulnerability is seldom easy, but personal fear melts in the presence of the overwhelming power and glory of our God. He is the One who is doing the work. It is our honor to be a part of His rescue team.

Peace, be still.

The outcome ultimately lies with the Infinite.

Chapter 11

#BandUnbroken

When the snows fall and the white winds blow, the lone wolf dies but the pack survives.

—George R. R. Martin

The ocean was bitterly cold that morning. Each wave brought more agony as the brackish water engulfed his head and filled his nose and mouth. The recruit lay flat on his back in the sand, his head facing the endless battery of waves that crashed mercilessly over him, soaking his already chilled body and pulling at his weary frame in an attempt to draw him back into the depths of the Pacific. His thin white T-shirt and military issue pants clung to his violently shivering form. They were no match for the numbing cold of the briny surf. Another wave, and more frigid seawater flooded his nose. He spluttered and gasped for air. *How much longer can this go on?* He lay in a long line of his fellow soldiers, their arms linked, each of them willing to take their body to the limit to earn the right to be called a Navy SEAL. The promise of that title propelled him and gave him hope. It was the link of interlocked arms and clenched fists that held off the pounding surf and kept him from sliding back into the sea, but it was the stronger bond, forged of suffering and exhaustion that kept him on that beach. He would not move. He would not give up. If the men around him had the will left to fight the desire to yield to the torturous elements of the sea line, then he could stick it out as well. Together they would endure. Together they would weather the storm of pain and cold. Together, a band unbroken.

> *And so, dear brothers and sisters, I plead with you to give your bodies to God because of all he has done for you. Let them be a living and holy sacrifice—the kind he will find acceptable. This is truly the way to worship him. (Romans 12:1 NLT)*

Repentance. Submission. Dependence.

This is the Gospel that Christ has called us to, to present ourselves as living sacrifices, holy and acceptable to God. The living sacrifice is the tricky part. It involves a constant state of submission, while we live in a body whose primal desire is to revolt in selfishness. It implies a willingness to repent from the daily failures and to rest in the hope of our great Savior. As the writer of Romans dives into this subject, it becomes abundantly clear that the difficulty of this task is not lost on him. Only fools go it alone. No sooner is the challenge of a life set apart splashed onto the page of his letter than he turns to the value of life in community. Paul addresses this need before the ink is even dry on his call to a Gospel-centered life. There are no self-sufficient followers of Christ. We need each other.

#LoneWolf

The frozen tundra of Alaska is a harsh and unforgiving place in the long winter months, especially for a wolf. During the summer, the abundance of small animals allows a solitary wolf to hunt with relative ease, but when winter arrives, most of the smaller prey go underground into hibernation. The only available food source becomes larger herd animals that are a daunting challenge even for the largest of the canine predators. This forces them to choose between survival and solitude. The pack rules. A full-grown caribou is no match for the might of the pack. Working together, wolves not only survive but thrive as a unified pack. Similarly, we all have times of relative summer in our lives, where problems are small and we have little trouble handling the bumps in the road of life alone. However, the course of human history tells us that winter is coming.

If the Gospel is truly about dependence, is should be no surprise that community is such a critical component of life in Christ. The importance of life lived in community is a common thread found throughout Scripture. Humankind's need for relationships—from God's commentary on Adam's solitude in the Garden of Eden to Christ's prayer in the garden of Gethsemane that the coming church would be unified—is clearly woven throughout Scripture. God's design for us is to live in community. In chapters 12 and 14 of Romans, Paul cautions against the pitfalls of alienation, but his words to the church in Ephesus are a perfect summary.

> *Instead, we will speak the truth in love, growing in every way more and more like Christ, who is the head of his body, the church. He makes the whole body fit together perfectly. As each part does its own special work, it helps the other parts grow, so that the whole body is healthy and growing and full of love. (Ephesians 4:15–16 NLT)*

Notice here that love is both at the start and the finish of this concept. Biblical community is not possible without a generous application of true, unselfish love in the face of the deeply flawed and imperfect collection of humans that make up the followers of Christ today. Love is not our natural default setting; selfishness is. Lasting love that is not dependent on the performance of others is a work of God in our hearts. This makes the rest of this passage plausible, connecting with others, growing in Him together, and using the gifts and abilities that He has given us as a blessing to others. Connect. Grow. Serve.

#Connect

The grueling ordeal of BUDs (basic underwater demolition training) that every potential SEAL applicant must endure is far more than just an agonizing test of physical and mental endurance. It is ultimately a breaking down of the individual and the forging of a fire-hardened team, unified against the elements and perils of the task ahead. With each new task, more stress is applied, until the pressure either breaks the aspiring soldiers or forces them to work as a fluid unit, unified by the shared suffering and exhaustion. Whether carrying a three-hundred-plus pound Zodiac over their heads while running on the beach or racing headlong with it into the breakers to battle against a never-ending line of crushing seven-foot waves, an individual's incredible strength and willpower are not the determining factors for success. One man cannot run for miles on a beach carrying a three-hundred-pound boat or paddle through a seven-foot breaker by himself. He needs a trustworthy team who trusts him in return. It is not sheer sadomasochistic deviousness that motivates the instructors to subject these men to such a grueling ordeal. Given that the SEAL team is such an elite unit, the relatively few who pass will likely be in combat operations with the ones who are training them. Their mentors understand that their very lives may depend on the ability of these soldiers to work under pressure together as a team.

Most people will never be thrown into the chaos of clandestine military operations, but our Creator understood that the stress and trouble of a life lived in pursuit of Christ is more than a match for any individual. We desperately need each other. Sharing grief, celebrating joy, and lending a hand where it is needed all require vulnerability and the ability to think outside of oneself with a true servant's heart. Our goal in community should not be, *What can I get for myself?* but rather, *How can I help support others around me?* Again and again in Scripture, we see this concept fleshed out. Bear one another's burdens. Be kind to one another and be tenderhearted, forgiving one another. Pray for one another. Love one another. (See Galatians 6:2; Ephesians 4:32; James 5:16; John 13:34.) Time after time, God tells us to live in community. In our individualized society where a traditionally communal resource such as water can be purchased in individual packaging, this flies in the very face of societal thinking. In a dog-eat-dog world, we need the power of the pack.

Where can we go to find community like this? Is

there some sort of Match.com for finding your pack? The answer is the same as it has been for the last two thousand years: the local church. Now before you stop reading, give me a moment to explain. I realize that some people have given up on the idea of church. Bad experiences, legalism, hypocrisy, and interpersonal conflict have driven countless Christians into the harsh winter of life to go it alone. I don't know your story, but I do know this: the Gospel Jesus came to share is based on rescuing deeply flawed and broken people from the prison of their own sin and selfishness. We need that deliverance on a daily basis as we continue to struggle in repentance, submission, and dependence. Wouldn't it logically follow that a church made up of these flawed and broken people humbly seeking Christ would still struggle at times with the selfishness that lies in every heart? There is no perfect church, and that is a good thing, because the second you or I walk through the door, we bring all of our own baggage with us. It is the very reason the Bible calls us to kindness, forgiving one another,[57] and encouraging or building each other up.[58] Connecting with people in a local church is not a passive process. It is not simply attending a service on Sunday. It is not just faithfully placing your weekly donation in the offering plate as it passes you by. It is not a passing acquaintance with a crowd of other people

57. Ephesians 4:32
58. 1 Thessalonians 5:11

who identify as Christian. This is where vulnerability and servanthood come into play. As we build trust with our cobelievers and obey the Savior's command to carry each other's burdens, it opens us up for potential heartbreak. C. S. Lewis said it best:

> *To love at all is to be vulnerable. Love anything and your heart will be wrung and possibly broken. If you want to make sure of keeping it intact you must give it to no one, not even an animal. Wrap it carefully round with hobbies and little luxuries; avoid all entanglements. Lock it up safe in the casket or coffin of your selfishness. But in that casket, safe, dark, motionless, airless, it will change. It will not be broken; it will become unbreakable, impenetrable, irredeemable. To love is to be vulnerable.[59]*

So many people feel as though the local church has failed them, and in reality, it has failed us all at one time or another. It is made up of flawed people, and sometimes it is the very process of learning to coexist and rely on our brothers and sisters in Christ in all their inadequacies and failings that helps shape us into His image.

Make time. Our culture moves at a thousand miles an hour. Busy schedules, long hours at work, kids' sporting events, school, and a myriad of other activities fight for time and energy in our lives. It all comes down to priorities.

---

59. C. S. Lewis, *The Four Loves* (C. S. Lewis Pte. Ltd., 1960), Used by permission.

Taking time for relationships is tougher than it seems, but the alternative is far worse. God is a relational being, and He designed us to be the same way. We all need deeper relationships to fully realize the life that God has intended for us. The default in our world is hundreds of acquaintances but few if any meaningful friendships in which we can pull back the carefully manicured facade that we work so hard to maintain. Substantial bonds like this take time to develop but are critical to life according to the Gospel.

#Grow

My daughters love bedtime stories. Almost every night, the process of selecting just the right one is a critical part of our routine. It can be the difference between tears and laughter, and the right to be the one to choose it is often a hotly contested debate. *Winnie the Pooh*, *The Cat in the Hat*, and *Go, Dog, Go!* are pitted against various illustrated Bible stories and classics like *Robin Hood* and *Sleeping Beauty*. Often, the girls imagine themselves as the characters, ruling their kingdoms as beautiful princesses or bravely fighting monsters. In one of those stories is a unique creature, a common frog, who was once a great prince. Spoiler alert: the climax of the plot is that a princess kisses him, and he is instantly transformed back into a handsome prince. Wouldn't it be wonderful if spiritual maturity worked the same way? One touch from the hand of the Messiah would instantly transform us into the perfect image of Christ. No more sin. No more selfishness. Only humility and love would remain. Sadly, that is not the case. In chapter 9 of this book, "#IntotheFire," we examined this process. Even the writer of Romans struggled.

> *I have discovered this principle of life—that when I want to do what is right, I inevitably do what is wrong. (Romans 7:21 NLT)*

Our transformation into maturity is not instantaneous by any means. It is a process woven together by study of the Word, prayer, character development, and obedience, in the spirit of repentance, submission, and dependence. Sometimes it can be easy for us to focus on things like personal devotions, our prayer life, or our walks with God, but we need to think of "body growth" as well, not just personal growth. Let me explain.

There are over two hundred species that bear the general name of army ant. Ants can be found all over the earth, except for the cold of the Arctic/Antarctic and the frigid peaks of the tallest of mountains. Army ants, however, are a force to be reckoned with.

> *When it comes to the art of war, it's army ants that will make you break into a cold sweat. Armored tough, with machete jaws, these masterful fighters hack and dice prey vastly larger than themselves by acting in*

numbers beyond easy comprehension. Imagine hordes
of spear-wielding humans at a wooly mammoth's feet.
That's the scale of army ant operations when they're
attacking a tarantula or scorpion. Army ant colonies
succeed at making tens of thousands such kills each day.[60]

These ants are amazing, considering a single ant apart
from its swarm is little more than a snack for most of the
other small creatures in its territory. So small, so vulnerable, yet when the combined might of an entire colony is
unleashed, even large animals avoid confrontation. This is
the power of the unified body of Christ. We were made to
thrive in community. We all play a part in that. Finding a
local church to call home is much more than finding one
that can meet your needs. It is finding a church that needs
you and committing to grow together and use the talents
and proficiencies that the Creator has carefully designed
you with.

And let us consider how to stir up one another to love
and good works, not neglecting to meet together, as is
the habit of some, but encouraging one another, and
all the more as you see the Day drawing near. (He-
brews 10:24–25 ESV)

We are to invest in growing each other. In the human
body, if one part is weak, the others often soon fail as well,

---

60. "Ants," *National Geographic*, August 2006, http://ngm.nationalgeographic
.com/2006/08/army-ants/moffett-text/3.

overworking to compensate.

So how do I know if I'm really growing as part of a body? In the ant world, there are two factors scientists look at to determine the health of a colony, and those two factors provide some very helpful insights into the health and maturity of a local church as well. The first is the community footprint of the hive. In a thriving colony, the effects of its presence can be felt significantly in the surrounding area. The population of small animals is dramatically reduced. Non-army ants and spiders, lizards, snakes, and frogs all fall prey to the marauding ant horde. If the church body that you are a part of is not having a significant effect on its surrounding community, that should concern you. The second health indicator is reproductive success, both for the colony itself and periodic colonies that spin off from the original. We are called as Christians not just to "win souls" or make conversions but to make disciples. Five times in Scripture, in the five Great Commission passages, Christ gives us explicit orders as to what is to be our main objective: make disciples.

> *Therefore, go and **make disciples** of all the nations, baptizing them in the name of the Father and the Son and the Holy Spirit. Teach these new disciples to obey all the commands I have given you. And be sure of this: I am with you always, even to the end of the age. (Matthew 28:19–20 NLT, emphasis added)*

Our main focus ought to be very clear—we are to make disciples. Reproduce reproducers. We are not attempting to moralize the masses but rather to be tools of the Creator to guide their hearts back to Him and allow the Gospel to change them from the inside out.

Spiritual growth in modern times is big business. Handy devotionals, compelling speakers, sold-out conferences, and ten-step plans to fix your spiritual life are commonplace. We have access to more preaching through recorded media than ever before, and there is never a shortage of spiritual self-help books and articles. There are spiritual checklists, spiritual growth guides, daily calendars with Scripture verses, and convenient daily e-mails sent straight to your inbox if you subscribe. Is this what Jesus had in mind when He instructed His band of followers to make disciples of the nations? I doubt it, although none of the things I listed above are inherently bad. Most of them can serve as useful tools in the pursuit of spiritual maturity, but they are not the main point. Like Paul says in 1 Corinthians 3:6, God is the only one who can bring growth. It is our job to cling to the Gospel each day in repentance, submission, and dependence, both individually and as a united body of believers. Growth, whether personal or corporate, takes time and effort. It would be great if after we accept Christ we are immediately transformed into His likeness, but that is not the case. As a body, life in community allows us to push one another onward in this pursuit.

I'm not a huge fan of shopping at the mall. For me, it is a necessary evil, a means to an end. Navigating the kiosks hawking everything from perfume to bathtub retrofits and fending off determined salespeople bent on peddling their wares is not something I enjoy. My wife, on the other hand, loves it. Shopping energizes her, and she excels at it. Shopping for a few things can turn into an all-morning quest for the perfect pair of pants. I just want to get in and get out. In this massive conglomeration of stores and food vendors, there is a shining monolith for all who just want to find their target and make their escape. It stands in a central location and holds the vital information necessary for a novice shopper to find their way in the chaos. A large freestanding backlit map with a giant, illustrated, color-coded floor plan of the mall points the way to freedom. It all starts with a small but helpful box on the map that states, "You are here."

Wouldn't it be great to have a map like that for our lives? Imagine a chart that plots the course of every decision, the solution to every problem, the answer to every question, the path to spiritual maturity and fulfillment. The sheer complexity would be staggering. We would need more than just a map—we would need a guide. That, at its core, is what discipleship is all about. We all need someone to help us navigate through life. We need someone who has already been where we are going to help us avoid the pitfalls and guide us through the tough times. That is discipleship. This is why Christ is so passionate about the idea of disciple making. His plan to grow the church is built on the back of interpersonal relationships. One person helps another. Everyone needs someone in their life as a mentor, and everyone needs to be mentoring someone else. There are always people farther along their spiritual journey than you, and there are always people who could use the experience and spiritual knowledge you possess to help them on their way. Sometimes the reason a good mentor is so hard to find is the ones who could be doing the mentoring are insecure about their own abilities. Here is the problem. Spiritual mentorship is a work of the Holy Spirit through us. God equips us for the task He appoints us to. Insecurity points to a misperception that the mentor is wholly responsible for the growth; but in reality, only God can enable someone to grow and mature. Helping a person plot a course through life through a personal relationship is a mission that all Christians are called to, and everyone needs a person or people in their life to return the favor.

#Serve

The rain fell in sheets as we drove. I leaned forward to peer through the windshield as the wipers did their best to clear the relentless torrents of water obscuring my view of the highway. Interstate 287 around New York City on Memorial Day weekend in heavy traffic was not my idea of a good time, but my wife, our kids, and I were on the way to an engagement of the utmost importance: my baby sister was getting married. So far, so good. We had plenty of gas, and the kids were quiet. But the hulking form of semi-trucks and their blinding spray made driving conditions less than optimal. The sooner we arrived at our destination, the better. I pushed the gas pedal to pass one of the clouds of mist created by the lumbering behemoths, and to my dismay, nothing happened. I looked down at the dash to see what the problem could be, but everything seemed normal. I tried again with the same result. The engine revved, but our SUV was gradually slowing down. My heart sunk. *Not now. Not here.* As I guided our vehicle to the much-too-small-to-be-safe shoulder, I already knew we were in for a long night. Our transmission was shot, and we were going nowhere on our own.

Transmissions are very important. They take the power of an engine and convert it into usable energy to propel a vehicle forward. The best engine in the world is just a massive hunk of metal without a gearbox to connect its muscle to the drive shaft and wheels. In our vehicle, we had lost that connection, and it stranded us in a bad place at a bad time. Spiritual growth in community is like that engine. Growing in Christ is great, but if that growth doesn't translate into a transformed heart and a life that pours itself out in service, there is a disconnect somewhere indicating that our spiritual "transmission" is broken. Someone may have what he or she thinks is an incredible prayer life, deep and meaningful times of study in the Word, and access to thought-provoking Bible teaching, and be able to recite verse after verse from memory . . .but if his or her life does not show an active interest in serving others, both inside the church and out, something is desperately wrong. When relationships are built and lives are transformed, service and ministry are natural results.

The mission is clear. The need for all of us to get involved is critical. Sometimes the hardest part is just understanding how to begin. So where do we start? If we truly want to be effective in serving those around us, both in the Church and in the community, we need to know two things.

1. We need to figure out what we are able to do, what we can bring to the table.

My heart goes out to children who are born with heart defects, but I obviously am not going to don scrubs and walk into a pediatric operating room in hopes of surgically repairing a new baby's faulty heart valve. I'm not a surgeon. I don't even play one on TV. I have spent a good portion of my life in the IT field. At one point, I worked for a large hospital in Virginia. I may not have been able to operate on a faulty valve, but when the computer system in the OR was malfunctioning, I was one of the team who would be called for help. God has created us all differently for a reason. Your specific gifts and abilities are desperately needed in the world and the Church. Do what you are good at.

2. We need to find out what the people around us actually need.

This can be tougher than it sounds. It requires the ability to listen. It necessitates the building of a trust relationship. Many times, well-meaning people have created more chaos than stability by barging into a situation and trying to "fix it" without first taking the time to listen and learn what the needs truly are. We need to know two things: *This is what I can do. This is what the people around me actually need.* At the intersection of these two things is the goal we need to work toward.

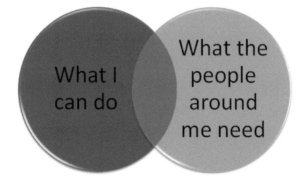

Love God. Love others. Taking an active role in serving those around you, both in the body of Christ and the society we live in, is one of the most concrete ways we can fulfill both of those commands at once. If a person professes to believe the Gospel that Jesus taught and serving others is not a main part of his or her life, something is deeply wrong. James says it best in the first chapter of the letter he wrote to the early church:

> *But be doers of the word, and not hearers only, deceiving yourselves. For if anyone is a hearer of the word and not a doer, he is like a man who looks intently at his natural face in a mirror. For he looks at himself and goes away and at once forgets what he was like. (James 1:22–24 ESV)*

The waves of life can be brutal. They keep coming. If you don't feel like you are drowning now, just wait; it will come. Sickness, grief, pain, and exhaustion come at us like the icy waves of a merciless ocean. Life overwhelms us. We desperately need the interlocking arms of fellow believers to keep us grounded and give us the will to keep fighting. Without the God-designed connection to other believers, relationships to push us toward Him, and the active service holding up those around us, we are doomed to be driven and tossed by the waves of life. Connect. Grow. Serve. Without them, sustained repentance, submission, and dependence are almost impossible.

Chapter 12

#RulesofEngagement

Perhaps travel cannot prevent bigotry, but by demonstrating that all people cry, laugh, eat, worry, and die, it can introduce the idea that if we try and understand each other, we may even become friends.

—Maya Angelou

For me, flying is a necessary evil. I understand that many people enjoy it. In fact, some people make a good living jetting about the country in a giant metal tube. However, I am not one of them. Interestingly enough, I am writing these words at 37,808 feet above sea level, on a 737 bound for Orlando. When you think about it, flying is an incredible experience. Man has only been airborne for a tiny fragment of history. The speed at which we can travel on the wings of a commercial airliner is amazing. My current flight is a little under two hours at a speed of over 500 mph, but had I traveled the same distance by car, it would have lasted over fifteen hours, with no bathroom stops! Trips that take days or even weeks by car or boat are condensed into mere hours. This is why I fly, despite the inconveniences. It isn't the motion sickness from potential turbulence on the route. Readily available over-the-counter medications take care of that. It isn't the need to arrive hours early for your flight, or long wait times standing in a line to have your belongings checked at a security point and your personal space invaded by a helpful TSA officer. I can understand the thinking behind those things. It isn't even the knee-crushing, cramped seating that is clearly not designed for a person who is over six feet tall. For me, the real problem is being trapped in a confined space with random people for hours at a time, at the mercy of screaming children and inattentive (or semi-helpless) parents, or rude inebriated passengers who hit the airport bar just a little too hard before takeoff, or back-of-seat kickers with restless feet, cramped and smelly restrooms, inescapable body odor, and the list goes on. Flying is a small but potent slice of the perils of living in a society with no opportunity for withdrawal.

A society, as defined by Wikipedia, is a group of people involved in persistent social interaction, or a large social group sharing the same geographical or social territory. A society has benefits that are not available to isolated individuals. At the very least, we each don't have to spend the bulk of our time hunting or farming all of our own food. Specialists in various fields are enabled to thrive and provide goods and services for the masses. Society at its best is an incredibly complex organism, and when all parts are working at maximum potential, the potential is virtually limitless, but what's the cost?

#EatMorChiken

Dan Cathy is arguably one of the most prolific chicken slingers of all time. His father Truett, founded a small fast food restaurant named Chick-fil-A. In 2014, they celebrated fifty years of selling chicken and have served over 3.2 billion sandwiches since 1964. In 2001 Dan succeeded his father as the president, in the year Chick-fil-A opened its one thousandth location. The business continued to be an enormous success story. Everything was going swimmingly, until one fateful day, June 16, 2012, Dan Cathy shared some of his personal convictions about marriage.[61] On a popular radio show, Cathy stated:

> *I think we are inviting God's judgment on our nation when we shake our fist at Him and say, "We know better than you as to what constitutes a marriage." I pray God's mercy on our generation that has such a prideful, arrogant attitude to think that we have the audacity to define what marriage is about.*

This statement brought down a firestorm of anger and resentment from the LBGTQ community. Social media

---

61. *Wikipedia*, s.v. "Chick-fil-A Same-Sex Marriage Controversy," last modified July 11, 2017, https://en.wikipedia.org/wiki/Chick-fil-A_same-sex _marriage_controversy

exploded with calls for a boycott and thinly veiled threats toward the fast food company. Proponents for the hotly contested issue of gay marriage were livid. In an attempt to calm the uproar, Dan Cathy had a second interview with a biweekly newspaper for the Southern Baptist Convention in North Carolina and gave this statement:

"We are very much supportive of the family—the biblical definition of the family unit. We are a family-owned business, a family-led business, and we are married to our first wives. We give God thanks for that. . . . We want to do anything we possibly can to strengthen families. We are very much committed to that," Cathy emphasized. "We intend to stay the course," he said. "We know that it might not be popular with everyone, but thank the Lord, we live in a country where we can share our values and operate on biblical principles."[62]

Things only got worse. Several colleges and universities launched efforts to ban or remove Chick-fil-A from their campuses. Gay rights organizations organized protests; news outlets had a field day; and on August 15 of that year, one very disturbed individual attempted to storm the Washington, DC, offices of the Family Research

---

62. K. Allan Blume, " 'Guilty as charged,' Dan Cathy says of Chick-fil-A's stand on faith," *Biblical Recorder.* July 2, 2012, quoted in *Wikipedia*, s.v. "Chick-fil-A Same-Sex Marriage Controversy, last modified July 11, 2017, https://en.wikipedia.org/wiki/Chick-fil-A_same-sex_marriage_controversy

Council, a noted opponent of gay marriage, with a 9mm handgun, a box of ammo, and a bag of fifteen Chick-fil-A sandwiches in an unsuccessful effort to kill as many people as possible. A security guard was wounded in the incident, but there were no casualties.

No matter what you think about the legality or morality of same-sex marriage, the very fact that these two statements from Cathy about his personal viewpoints made national news and garnered such a considerable backlash is significant. Twenty years ago, these statements wouldn't have even been a blip on the societal radar. Today they are the kindling for a blistering firestorm of public outrage. Matt Chandler says it well:

> *We live in a world now, that to disagree with anyone's lifestyle means we either hate them or are afraid of them.*
>
> *The church is being pushed into the margins, and it's not easy for Christians to go from favor to being perceived as fools in a couple of decades, to go from honorable to be seen as bigots.*[63]

How do we exist, even thrive, in a society that does not share our values and beliefs? The church in first-century Rome was no stranger to the challenges of push-back against the teachings of the Gospel. The emperor

---

63. Matt Chandler, "God's Glory as Our Courage" (sermon). Used with permission.

of Rome at the time of Paul's letter to the Romans was none other than Nero, one of the most infamously brutal persecutors of the early church in recorded history. Tacitus, a famed Roman historian, documented some of the terrible things that were done to Christians by Nero,[64] including death by ravenous wild dogs, crucifixion, and even dipping them in oil and using them as human torches to light his royal gardens. Paul was acutely aware of these things, and in the last few chapters of his letter to the Romans, he lays out a three-pronged strategy to deal with this very complex issue of how to relate to a society that does not hold the same values: Obey authority. Love others. Stay pure.

No matter what side of the aisle you land on politically, we have all had times when we are immensely dissatisfied, even frustrated with the governing policies and oversight in our homelands. Unfair treatment, obscene amounts of waste, unbridled corruption, unpopular policy, and a complete disconnect with the people leaders are responsible for are some of the common themes of governmental dissent. Compounded by our innate dislike of being told what to do and how to do it, it is very easy to see how mountains of resentment are quickly formed. Paul tackles this first when he writes:

Everyone must submit to governing authorities. For

64. Paul Barnett, *Jesus & the Rise of Early Christianity: A History of New Testament Times* (Downers Grove, IL: InterVarsity Press, 2002), 30.

all authority comes from God, and those in positions of authority have been placed there by God. So anyone who rebels against authority is rebelling against what God has instituted, and they will be punished. (Romans 13:1–2 NLT)

These are strong words, especially considering the ruler at the time of this writing. Obey authority. It's pretty clear. Our role as followers of the Gospel is not one of defiance and discord to the leadership in our society but as law-abiding citizens of our temporary residences. We are members of the divine rescue team first, and remembering that our true citizenship lies in the eternal home awaiting us will help to recalibrate our perspective, even through times of great trouble and oppression. Does this mean that we are to engage in or condone things God has clearly defined as sin in His Word? No. From the Hebrew midwives' refusal to slaughter the babies of their countrymen at the order of the Pharaoh,[65] to the three brave young men who defied the Babylonian dictator's command to bow down and worship at the gigantic golden statue of himself,[66] the Bible shows us that there are appropriate times for civil dissent. It is interesting to note that these times of disobedience were not protests of a current decree but rejection of a personal act that would

---

65. Exodus 1:17

66. Daniel 3

defy God's law in their own lives. Many countries today allow for their populace to have a say in the policies that govern their daily lives, and this provides an opportunity for us to be light and salt in a world that may not share our values. Paul even goes as far as validating the concept of taxation, a timeless source of resentment and rage, as he writes:

> *Pay your taxes, too, for these same reasons. For government workers need to be paid. They are serving God in what they do. Give to everyone what you owe them: Pay your taxes and government fees to those who collect them, and give respect and honor to those who are in authority. (Romans 13:6–7 NLT)*

This follows the same line of reasoning Jesus gives when He tells His followers to give to Caesar what is Caesar's. Don't get distracted by the squabbles over earthly governance. Fix your mind on the eternal and the things that will last forever.

The second prong of Paul's direction to the Romans (and us) about existing in society revolves around purity. This is not the meticulous, competitive checklist morality of the Pharisees in his day. It is not a pride-based system for Christians to prove how "holy" they are and use their own perceived goodness as a gavel to condemn those around them. Those were the people who Jesus condemned the most while He was on the planet. Paul is calling us to a life of submission and dependence.

> *Because we belong to the day, we must live decent lives for all to see. Don't participate in the darkness of wild parties and drunkenness, or in sexual promiscuity and immoral living, or in quarreling and jealousy. Instead, clothe yourself with the presence of the Lord Jesus Christ. And don't let yourself think about ways to indulge your evil desires. (Romans 13:13–14 NLT)*

Sin clouds the mind and can destroy the impact we can have as members of the divine rescue team. It's not just what you do; it goes deeper, to the thought patterns we allow ourselves to think. We are masters of rationalization. Given enough time, we can convince ourselves that almost anything "isn't so bad." Sin breaks our fellowship with God and hurts us many times both physically and spiritually. The good news is that there is always forgiveness in response to repentance. The more we can understand the way God forgives, the more connected to Him we will be.

Going back to the idea of God's timeless forgiveness, let's look at it this way. You have done something terribly hurtful to your best friend. In the aftermath, you sincerely apologize, acknowledging your actions and asking for forgiveness. Like a good friend, your request is met with mercy and compassion, and the relationship is restored.

Only a few days later, the same hurt is inflicted again and the process repeats, this time a little more awkwardly. Again and again this happens, each time growing more difficult to repair the brokenness, and each time shame builds, making it harder and harder to broach the topic of forgiveness. That is how human forgiveness works, but God is much different. The I AM exists at all points of the timeline. That means when you ask Him to forgive, He not only knows about every other time you have fallen short, and every single time you will break your relationship with Him in the future, but *He is there*. He truly forgives. There is no time at which we should be reticent to come to Him with our failure. Like Adam and Eve hiding like children in the garden, as though the Eternal Infinite is not already acutely aware of their actions, we play at futile attempts to hide our sin from a God who witnesses all of history in an instant and knows the depths of our souls. He has made a way for reconciliation through the suffering of His Son, and the only thing impeding that is our own pride. We are called to purity, not in our own strength but in the power He gives us. We are called to daily repent, submit, and depend on Him. This is the greatest news ever. This is life lived in light of the Gospel.

#AllaboutMe

My knees are killing me. If the person sitting in front of me leans her seat back any farther, my kneecaps are going to be permanently relocated. The stewardess glances at me sympathetically as she trundles by with her cart of pretzels and bottled water. To be honest, my plight is relatively tame compared with some of the pictures I've seen of weary travelers dealing with the outrageous behavior of their fellow airline passengers. Smelly bare feet, propped up on the seat in front of them; personal hygiene deficiencies that would gag a maggot; sprawling sleepers who have no respect for the edges of their personal space; and inebriated airport bar patrons who either don't know their own limitations or don't care, all make for some very uncomfortable travel conditions. Our nature at its core excels at selfishness. *Who cares about the people around me, as long as I'm comfortable?* The Gospel is the antithesis to this. It is humility in a world of self-promotion. It is sacrifice when everyone else is fighting for their "fair share." It is love for others when culture preaches self-absorption. This is the third point of Paul's advice for existing in an adversarial culture.

> *Owe nothing to anyone—except for your obligation to love one another. If you love your neighbor, you will fulfill the requirements of God's law. (Romans 13:8 NLT)*

This is the basis for the Gospel. God loved us so much that He set His own comfort aside to meet our needs. We were ugly, broken, and covered in sin. He was perfect and holy. His love was our redemption, and we are called to that same love. When people hear the words "follower of Christ," the first descriptive word to come to mind should not be *judgmental*. We are called to love those around us, sacrificially and without reward. It's tough to love someone else when you are consumed with seeking your own comfort. In a day and age where everyone is clamoring for their own personal rights and privilege, Christians need to be the ones willing to set their own wants aside to meet the needs of others. We need to be grace-filled, pouring our lives out for the hurting and oppressed, just as our Savior did. We need to be good listeners, giving others an opportunity to find solace for their pain, quick to extend a hand to those who are ostracized by society. We need less picketing and protesting and more people helping to pick up the pieces of the broken lives around us.

We are called to the rescue team, to be messengers of the best news of all time. This is our role in society now. Our primary directive is the dissemination of that news. We need to be clear on that. We are not the morality police. After all, what good does it do to pressure others into moral behavior if they are still spiritually dead in sin? We are to be salt and light, illuminating the path to

Christ and His finished work of redemption. Many long hours have been spent on campaigns and boycotts calling for this policy or against that particular sin, but only God can change hearts. The enemy of the best is the good, and too often we waste time chasing after solutions that can't offer the lasting change of men and women made alive in Christ. Our movement is not a political one. It is an unstoppable tide of love and grace, led by Love Himself, to a world that is desperate for liberation from the bondage and darkness we have lived with for so long.

How do we deal with a society that doesn't share the same values as we do? How do we coexist in a world that is many times diametrically opposed to our core belief system? Obey authority. Stay pure. Above all else, love God and love our neighbors. We may be stuck on this ride surrounded with unruly passengers who, at times, seem bent on the destruction of our faith, or at least our sanity, but our great Savior has given us everything we need to live godly lives of service to those around us, and the incredible opportunity to be a part of the extraordinary rescue plan He has set in place for all of humanity. There may be some turbulence ahead, and our journey will most likely be filled with the unexpected, but His strength is enough.

Conclusion
#AllIn

The Gospel has one object, producing in us sinners a condition that will satisfy the heart of our God.
  —WATCHMAN NEE, *THE NORMAL CHRISTIAN LIFE*

The playing field is leveled. We all stand fairly condemned by a righteous and holy God, who is in all ways the perfect Judge; but in His divine love for us, He has made a way to restore the broken relationship with Himself that we severed. From the garden to the cross, from the empty tomb to the imminent return of the rightful King of all creation, the Gospel is God's divine rescue plan for all humanity. It's a story about true Love overcoming all odds. It is the forsaking of self and dedication to sacrificial love for others. It is repentance from the sin that is always present, submission to the design that our Creator has laid out, and daily dependence on Him to change us from the inside out. The Gospel is not just about a one-time decision to escape judgment—it is about new life. This life is radically different from much of the religious culture that identifies as Christian. It's lived in a spirit of constant repentance for the ongoing failures of an endless battle with sin. It is a continual submission to God's commands, not in an effort to win favor, but an acknowledgment of His wisdom and love for us. It is a perpetual admittance of our inability to transform ourselves, and an unceasing dependence on the only one who can change us from the inside out. The Gospel leaves no room for fence-sitters. We are either on the rescue team or part of the problem. There are no solo operators. Either we accept our helpless state and fully depend on the remedy Christ has provided, or we try to fix things our own way with catastrophic results. There is no life without Christ. He provides us with everything we need for life and godliness.[67] It is not self-righteous, judgmental indignation. It is a call to follow in the steps of the greatest servant who ever lived, to be light in a culture of darkness. As Dietrich Bonhoeffer, a pastor who lived through the horrors of Nazi Germany, once said:

When Christ calls a man, He bids him come and die.[68]

Paul understood this concept better than most. He spoke of his own life being poured out as a drink offering for the purpose of this divine rescue plan.[69] He was no stranger to suffering. As he dictates the final words of his

---

67. 2 Peter 1:3

68. Dietrich Bonhoeffer, *The Cost of Discipleship.* New York: MacMillan, 1959.

69. 2 Timothy 4:6; Philippians 2:17

letter to the Romans, death is closing in quickly. Paul had held nothing back. He had finished playing the hand he was dealt, and he was all-in.

#MomentofTruth

Two aces. The cards burned in his hand. His pulse raced. For years, he had worked for this moment, played countless hands of back-room poker, winning some, losing many more. He had finally scraped together the cost of admission for this prestigious tournament. He had patiently and deliberately hung around as his competitors were eliminated, and now this was the hand he had been waiting for. He stared solemnly at the table, careful to hide any hint of excitement that would give away his position. The room around him was filled with hushed chatter. The bright lights shone like the desert sun on a parched wasteland. Spectators intently watched his every move. This was the final table at the biggest event in the game. The player glanced around the table to see the now-empty chairs of others that had fallen one by one as the night progressed. There were now only two. It was now or never. He pushed his entire pile of clay poker chips toward the center of the table and swallowed hard. There was no turning back now. He was all in.

So what will you do now? Will your understanding

of the Gospel recalibrate your way of life, or will it be relegated to the intellectual scrap heap of self-help books and good advice untaken? Will you continue to try to make your own way, or will you let the good news of the Gospel lead you into the abundant life that Christ offers? Make no mistake, this is no one-time push of all your chips to the center of the table of life. It is a daily struggle to repent, submit, and depend on the finished work of our Savior.

This is the *#Gospel*.

ABOUT THE AUTHOR

Daniel Rice is the founder of #Gospel, an organization created to bring the Gospel to the current generation in a way that syncs with their culture and uniqueness. Before #Gospel, Daniel spent ten years on staff with Calvary Church in Lancaster, Pennsylvania, working with small groups, young adults, and students. He and his wife, Melissa, have five children.

If You Liked This Book, You'll Also Like...

#Truth
by Josh McDowell

This brand-new devotional from Josh McDowell unpacks spiritual truths that inspire, challenge, and fuel young people every day of the year—from January 1 to December 31. Practical and relevant, each month of devotional readings shares a common theme—from January: The Truth That God Exists to December: The Truth About Christ's Return.

Paperback / 978-1-63409-975-2 / $16.99

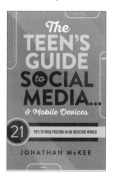

The Teen's Guide to Social Media and Mobile Devices
by Jonathan McKee

Jonathan McKee shares helpful tips for today's teens and tweens navigating the digital world. With tips like *Nothing you post is temporary* and *Don't post pics you wouldn't want Grandma, your boss, and Jesus seeing! (Jesus is on Insta, you know!)*, Jonathan's approach is refreshingly honest and humorous, as one who knows teens and understands the way they think, providing information for them to make informed decisions and challenging them in a way that encourages and inspires. . .without belittling.

Paperback / 978-1-68322-319-1 / $12.99

THE SELF-AWARE PARENT

19 LESSONS FOR GROWING WITH YOUR CHILDREN

CATHY CASSANI ADAMS,
LCSW, PCI CERTIFIED PARENT COACH

To Mom, Dad, Chris, and Peg for my beginning.
To Todd, Jacey, Camryn, and Skylar for my now.

Table of Contents

Acknowledgments

Thanks to my parents, John and Judy Cassani; my sister, Christine McFadden; and my aunt, Peg Jividen. I am extremely grateful for my upbringing and the closeness of my family. Thanks for the love and thanks for always being there.

Thanks to Drew, Maddie, and Max McFadden for being my home before I had a home of my own.

Thanks to the Adams family and the Ghilarducci family for the love, support and generosity.

To my parent coach and spiritual advisor Linda PetersenSmith for introducing me to ME. Thanks for holding the space so I could get out of my head and into my heart.

To all of my wonderful friends, especially Andrea Robinson, Nancy Bird, Jenny Zabrocki, Amy Clanton, Meghan Lee, Meg Bradley, Amy Connell Donohue, Elisabeth Shake, Amy Hearst, Jerry Evans, and Brian Kappel. You give me roots, love, and most importantly humor.

A special thanks to Monisha and Chris Lozier, Lara and Chris Forte, and Jessica Rappe for the companionship that keeps me aware and grounded. Thanks for knowing who I am and supporting me as I grow and change.

Thanks to my playgroup, Jen Krichbaum, Jacki Quinn, Jen Hughes, Cicely Jones, Karyn Sathy, Jennie Cannek, and Deb Casey for surrounding me during the early days of parenthood.

To Anne Kaplan, Mary Rose Hennessy, John Conrath, Bob Sheets, and all of the staff at Business and Industry Services. Thanks for guiding me in the early stages of my career and for leading me back to teaching.

To my supervisors Marena Sabo, Colleen Cicchetti, Karen Pierce, and the milieu staff at Children's Memorial Hospital, Partial Hospitalization Program. Thank you for the education, professional experience, and friendship.

Thanks to Gloria DeGaetano, founder of the Parent Coaching Institute, a visionary whose work makes an impact on families and society as a whole. Your supportive coaching model defines my professional identity and it allows me to work with energy and integrity.

Thanks to all my yoga teachers, especially Sarah and Stephanie Starnes, Ellie Taylor, and all of my friends in teacher training at Elmhurst Yoga Shala. I am inspired by your wisdom and I am grateful for the supportive community.

To all of my coaching clients and students, thanks for letting me learn and grow along side you.

Thanks to my writing group, Debra Gilbert Rosenberg and Carol Grandstaff, for all of the hours at Panera Bread and for encouraging me to write like I talk. Special thanks to my editor Melinda Copp who helped me turn the ideas in my head and six years of essays into a published book.

To my three beautiful girls Jacey, Camryn, and Skylar, for simply being who you are. Thank you for coming into my life and demonstrating what it means to be authentic. You are my teachers and my true loves.

Thanks to Todd for being my husband and best friend. Thanks for your thoughtful communication and willingness to listen as I analyze and interpret the meaning of everything. Thank you for your personal awareness and for making our family the center of your life. You are a man of integrity and you live from your heart. I am so blessed to live and parent by your side.

Somewhere, over the rainbow, skies are blue.
And the dreams that you dare to dream
Really do come true.

Lyrics from **Over the Rainbow**
written by Harold Arlen and E.Y. Harburg

Introduction

I was going to be a broadcast journalist. I watched the people on the nightly news and thought their work was exciting. They had important information to share and at the end of the day everyone tuned in to listen. I followed this path until my second year in college. I was sitting in a journalism class and I had an out-of-the-blue epiphany. *I want to be a teacher.* I came from a family of teachers, but until this moment I did not realize education was my path, too. A change in my major meant a lot more work, specifically summer classes and eighteen credit hours a semester. With this in mind I still felt compelled to make this shift and ended up with a teaching certification in elementary education.

I graduated during an economic downturn, so teaching jobs were limited. I moved to Chicago and eventually found a job teaching ESL and basic skills to adult students. This experience was profound because I found, although my job was to educate, these students needed a different kind of support. They had financial difficulties and struggles with work and family. I found myself listening to their experiences and offering whatever I could. This was not completely unfamiliar. Listening and supporting friends and family always felt natural to me. I was comfortable offering guidance or maybe a helpful story. I realized that instead of teaching basic skills, I wanted to teach life skills. I received my masters in social work and eventually became a licensed clinical social worker after doing my graduate experience at Children's Memorial Hospital. After completing my training I was offered the clinical educator/classroom teacher position in the Partial Hospitalization Program. My teaching certification gave me a foot in the door and after a few years I was offered a job as a child and family therapist in Child Psychiatry.

My first daughter was born a few years later and it was a huge shift for me. I decided to stay home with her and, somewhere in her first three months, I lost myself. I was overwhelmed by the challenge of parenthood and I didn't know who I was without my profession. I began writing about my experiences and searched for a way to work from home while taking care of my baby. I found the Parent Coaching Institute (PCI) and decided to go back to school to get my certification as a parent coach. The model resonated with me as a professional and as a parent because it focused on practicing self care, shifting attention to what was working, respecting a child's individuality, and practicing self awareness. As a therapist I can identify and diagnose a problem and as a coach I teach introspection and attention to strengths. By balancing these two ideologies I discovered an effective way to support parents and families.

Yoga is the physical manifestation of awareness and for me it offers personal and professional clarity. The universal principles of yoga focus on seeking balance but also accepting where you are today. Yoga can be demanding and challenging, but it also brings openness and inner peace. To me it is a perfect metaphor for parenting and this guided my decision to become a yoga teacher.

When I coach, teach, present, or give yoga instruction, I send the message that life and parenting are meant to be enjoyed. If I would have followed my initial intentions to become a broadcast journalist, my daily message might have been violence, fear, and world problems. My choice to share a positive message is not to deny that challenges exist, but to focus more of our energy on what feels good. Children's set point is joy and if we pay attention, they can help us return to that state of mind. Children are incredible teachers if we are willing to observe and listen.

The essays in this book are personal experiences, usually written because I was searching for a way to appropriately deal with a parenting issue and I needed verbal clarity on how to share my experiences with others. A few of these articles were published in *Chicago Parent* magazine and most of the others were published in my online parenting newsletter or blog.

I know that parenting can be a daunting job and the expectations are limitless. Children need to be kept physically safe and learn the laws and expectations of society. They need love, guidance, and nurturance so they grow up emotionally healthy; and they require education and support so they can eventually create a life of their own. We are expected to teach our children so many things, it is easy to forget that they are here to teach us as well.

Parenting is a phenomenal educational experience, and not just in terms of child-care. If one is open to it, parenting is like standing in front of a mirror. Raising children highlights your skills, but it will also point out your vulnerabilities. Things you have learned to hide or beliefs that don't serve you will rise to the surface. My first parenting awareness came immediately after I brought my first daughter home. Educational and work experiences had taught me that constant productivity equaled self worth. Caring for my daughter left little time for daily tasks, and I was unable to be productive in the way I had been in the past. I was forced to find a new kind of confidence as an individual and a mother, which required a great deal of patience and introspection. I allowed myself to grieve for my old life and I did a lot of work to figure out who I wanted to be as a parent. Motherhood brought out parts of me that I didn't know existed and it tested my ability to manage crises and deal with the unknown. Parenthood shifted the relationship with my spouse, my friends, and my family and it eventually became the focus of my profession. This was the beginning of self awareness through parenting.

Self awareness is a gift from our children because it's an opportunity to grow and become fully realized human beings. Parenting is grounding and it urges you to focus on what is most important in life – your relationships with others. Parenting is a lifelong commitment that requires you to work through challenges and be aware of what you bring to the relationships you create with your children.

Taking personal responsibility for your role in the parent-child relationship can be difficult because it is much easier to focus on your children's imperfections. Parents often seek my services because they have one "problem child" and they believe if this child would behave, the family would be stable. The child may have obvious behavior problems, but parents must examine their interactions and behavior with the child as well. Children give and receive love differently, and the parent's job is to find the best way to reach them. A child who is acting out may be trying to communicate something beyond their ability level.

With love and good intentions, parents often focus their energy on the wrong things. They want their children to have everything they didn't have, or they want them to have all of the right "stuff." They want their children to take all the right classes and they want them to say all the perfect things. The truth is much simpler. Children need to feel accepted for who they are, not just for what they do or how they look. They need to express themselves and they need you to listen and support them. They need your time and they need physical contact like holding hands or a hug. They need to know that you are taking care of yourself and finding your own happiness so they don't have to shoulder that burden. Children do not need things and gifts; they just need a healthy and trusting relationship with their parents. This is where confidence and happiness originates.

When parents realize that some of their choices have not been good ones, they lose confidence or feel guilt. Guilt is not something someone can give you; you make a choice to feel it. Guilt is a burden and an incredible waste of your valuable energy. Instead of identifying a problem and learning from the experience, guilt will tell you to carry the incident around and just feel bad about it. This is why it's important to balance self awareness with self acceptance. The whole point of life is to learn more about who you are and grow and learn from experiences. If you decide to endlessly beat yourself up every time you say the wrong thing or make a misstep, parenting is going to be a very long road. Learn how to apologize when necessary and accept who you are right now. Role model what it looks like to be aware, make changes, and continue on with grace.

Self awareness begins with very simple steps. Start by monitoring your mood when you are with your children. Are you carrying around stress and allowing your children to get the brunt of your frustration? I admit that I react much differently to my children's behavior based on my mood. If I am feeling good and they spill water, I might laugh and ask them to help me clean it up. If I am running late or frustrated with work and they spill water, I end up giving them a lecture about being careful and then grudgingly clean it up by myself. In the moment it is hard for me not to react this way, but with reflection I can see that my children did nothing but spill water and my mood dictated the severity of the situation.

If you are always in a hurry, assess your need to rush around and be busy. Children need activity, but they also need plenty of downtime. If you are not comfortable with downtime, address the issue so your children don't have to be on your fast-paced schedule. Children need time to process, relax, and reflect, and this doesn't mean time in front of the television. They need time for stillness, imagination, play, and individual time with you.

Downtime allows for limitless possibilities. Use the time to give your children a hug and allow them to pull away first. Play the game that you have been promising to play for the last year and the read the books that are sitting on the shelf. Sit outside or go for a nature walk. Just be present and available so your children can ask you questions and tell you stories.

Slowing down and heightening your awareness may help you realize that you need support or new parenting tools. Parenting is the most important job and the most difficult job on earth, yet so often parents feel embarrassed to ask for help or admit they are struggling. Every successful CEO and every great athlete has a coach or mentor; why does our society feel parenting needs to be done in isolation? Parents always tell me they will do anything for their children, but they often fail to take the first important steps. Take care of yourself first. Decide what you want to teach your children. Role model the behavior you teach your children. Learn effective discipline techniques and apply them consistently. Make the relationship with your children (and significant other) top priority, and ask for help when you need it.

Parenting books can offer a new perspective or a helpful idea, but a book should not be looked at as an all-knowing guide. A book is a reference to supplement your own parenting instincts. Child development books are helpful because they detail stages of development and provide typical age-appropriate behavior, but "advice" books can be confusing because they give ever-changing and often conflicting advice. This is because there is no one way to parent and you are the person that knows your children the best. I have three children and I have learned that I need to parent each of them a little differently. I have structure and boundaries and basic expectations, but I honor that each child and each day is different. Two of my children usually get up at 6:00, one likes to sleeps until 8:00. One child would rather spend time in the house, while the other two prefer to be outside. Jacey needs lots of hugs, Camryn wants to play games and help me clean, and Skylar wants me to hold my face and look me in the eye when she tells me stories. There is no right or wrong, these are just the ways they give and receive love. To parent effectively I need to focus on their needs rather than search for a definitive answer in a book.

Sharing personal stories and providing information (like the essays in this book) are an important part of my chosen profession, parent coaching. Telling stories develops trust and connection with a client and it normalizes common parenting experiences. A story can offer solutions, but it also opens up a conversation to investigate other possibilities. It allows a client to contemplate their family and belief system so they can make effective choices for their home.

The stories shared in this book were written over the course of six years and they are presented in the order in which they were written. You will notice that my writing style changed over time and the lessons became more personal and profound. I wrote an introduction for each essay as a reflection on the experience or to explain why the topic is so important for parents today.

As a self-aware parent you will realize that your child has his own reason for being here — and his own life to live. Instead of putting your hopes and dreams on your children, you will allow them to find their own hopes and dreams. Your children are not an extension of you. They have their own inner world and their own path. To parent effectively you may need to let go – let go of old patterns, let go of needing to control, let go of needing to be right all the time. Your children will let you know when it is time to look at these things – they are more than willing to tell you when you are holding on to tight. Children need to be held and kept safe, but they also need freedom to become who they are meant to be. It is a delicate balance and it is the definition of unconditional love.

The New Mom

As a new mom, I felt lost. I was unprepared for the identity shift and the intense emotional fluctuations. The experience was so profound it inspired my first article and the development of my New Moms Class. The class was an opportunity for women to share their early motherhood experiences and receive support and validation from each other.

New dads can feel just as lost when the baby comes home. Their wife is different, their home is different, and they often don't feel connected to an infant that constantly longs for mom. Communication, honesty, and support for each other are essential to navigate this new life as parents.

Lesson: *When you become a parent for the first time, it's important to grieve your life prior to baby. Acknowledge that life is different so you can fully embrace your new role. Once you do this, you can fully appreciate the amazing gift that you have been given.*

༄

Is motherhood what you expected? It's okay if it isn't. People might try to tell you what you should feel or how lucky you are, but it is normal to feel overwhelmed. Becoming a mother is a life altering experience, and we tend to stay quiet about the tough times. Throughout your pregnancy you know that your life will be different once the baby is born, but you don't know what that means until it happens. Motherhood can bring elation, guilt, tears, laughter, and a brand new outlook on life. If you are a new mom, know that the emotional swings and the sleep deprivation will eventually be under control, and that somewhere down the line, you will begin to feel comfortable with your new reality.

People will tell you to sleep when your baby sleeps, but for some reason you feel as if you should fold the laundry and write thank-you notes. People might offer to watch your baby for an hour or two, but you decline the offer because you fear outside germs or the possibility of a kidnapper breaking in while you are gone. These irrational fears are typical at the

1

beginning. The important thing to remember is that if you take care of yourself, you can better care for your baby. You need rest and energy to be the person who can rationally make choices for this human being. Becoming a martyr and doing it all alone can cause resentment and isolation. Ask for help and accept help when it is offered.

Taking care of yourself may also alleviate your desire to lash out at anyone who is showered or more rested—especially your partner. It became very clear to my husband that I needed time away from our first baby the day I exploded when he said he was going to Target. I said, "You are going to Target? I don't get to just *go* to Target anymore! I have to plan to go to Target! You are free to go to Target anytime you want and I am trapped!" It was clear that I desperately needed some time to myself. Understand that the foundation of your family is you and your partner. This foundation needs to be strong for everything else in the home to run smoothly. Bringing a new baby into your family will necessitate a lot of communication and possibly a few necessary breakdowns, but don't forget the importance of taking care of each other. Make it a goal to share your feelings with your partner and work as a team.

Having a baby changes how you live and how you think. Embrace the new person you are becoming and have confidence that this role will become more clear and comfortable in time. Find a new moms group so you can share frustrations and listen to experiences. Talk with friends about their early mothering experiences so they can assure you that things will calm down. As a mother your heart becomes bigger for your child, and it becomes bigger for the world. You feel more, worry more, love more, and see more. You have deeper compassion, more patience, more fear, and extreme gratefulness. You understand that everybody is someone's child, and everybody was once as innocent as your baby. The reality of motherhood may not be exactly what you expected, but it is still the experience of a lifetime.

My Tasks

An inevitable rite of passage for a new mom is finding a new definition for the word "productive." It can no longer mean how much you get done in a short amount of time because your time is no longer your own. In the first couple months with my daughter "productive" simply meant that I was able to take a shower. A child is born and so is a new set of rules on how to measure worth.

When I am with my children I am often stopped by older parents who say, "Enjoy this time, it goes so fast." I always appreciate these gentle reminders. The thrill of checking things off my list and accomplishing work-related tasks will probably always appeal to me, but another part of me has developed a deep appreciation for the ever-changing and often unpredictable life as mom.

Lesson: *As a parent you may need to redefine productivity. Parenting well necessitates slowing down, being present, and building a relationship.*

❦

As a working woman my worth was measured by my productivity. I had places to go and people to see. Completing tasks and reaching goals was the essence of my existence. I had a title, an office, and a purpose. I felt a sense of accomplishment at the end of the day and I felt worthy of my paycheck and my weekends. I knew who I was and I knew that all of my educational and previous work experiences had led up to this point. I had become who I had set out to be.

When I became a mother I had an identity crisis. I had no experience in this job and I was extremely insecure about my day-to-day experiences. Even if I created a task list it was almost impossible to cross things off—time was no longer my own. There was no predictability and no way to measure my productivity. I had stacks of parenting books all over the house and I was constantly calling more experienced mothers to alleviate my daily anxiety. I was a novice—I had started over. At 6:00 p.m. I would often wonder what I did all day. All I knew was that I was living on five hours of interrupted sleep and that I had kept my baby alive. Is that really all I had to show for myself?

Even when I was experiencing beautiful moments with my baby my mind would drift to her naptime when I would *really* get things done. While my baby slept I would accomplish the tasks that I deemed important. I would cross whatever I could off my list. I loved the natural high of getting things accomplished, but like a drug, it was never enough and I always wanted more. It often felt like I was just moving through the time with my baby so I could have more valuable time with my computer and my checklist. After all, this is how I had always measured the effectiveness of a day. I began to realize how detached I was from my new life. I was using an old set of rules and standards that did not work in my new situation. I no longer knew who I was or how to validate my importance.

After lots of time, intimate discussion, and personal contemplation I realized the distinct difference between work and parenting. At work you practice efficiency and demonstrate productivity, but when you parent you have to slow down and live in the moment. Effective parenting depends on becoming emotionally available and physically present with your child. Your worth is no longer measured by completed tasks and busy-ness; it is measured by picking up your child when she cries, having important conversation during dinner, and teaching your child why eating play dough is yucky.

My children are my teachers. Children only live in the present so I try to experience their world when we are together. For them, every experience is exciting and there is always something to learn. They repeat the same stories and they choose the same books over and over again. They enjoy unfolding freshly folded laundry, and building a tower and knocking it down is much more fun the tenth time. They have all the time in the world. At times my mind still drifts to time on my computer or the laundry that needs to be folded, but at least now I recognize these as second tier needs. Feeding, bathing, and putting my kids to bed are a great way to end the day.

Making the choice to slow down with my child is a major shift from my previous life and I might always be a work in progress. I have come to realize that part of parenthood is simply staying present enough to enjoy it. Parenting is now the first and most important task on the list, yet it's not something that I can actually complete. This is something I am learning to embrace and appreciate at the same time.

Talking about Feelings

I encourage all parents to pay attention to their children's feelings. I wrote this article after watching too many parents tell their children not to cry or get annoyed when their children demonstrate excitement. Feelings make us human, and releasing what we feel is necessary for emotional health. Helping a child identify feelings and then validating what they feel is an essential parenting skill. It's also important to help children find tools to deal with their feeling so they have the ability to comfort themselves.

Responding to a crying infant is the first acknowledgment of feelings—soothing a baby lets him know that you care and understand. In toddlerhood children begin to look for words to identify their feelings, especially strong emotions, like fear, anger, or sadness. These emotions can be scary for a child and they need someone they trust to normalize the experience.

Lesson: *Children need to release and talk about feelings. Allow your children to share what they are feeling and help them discover tools to deal with powerful emotions.*

❧

My daughter loves to play games, but she dislikes putting them away. Sometimes she whines as she picks up game pieces and cards off the floor. She often struggles as she tries to fold the game board correctly. To express how she feels, she throws a card and puts her head down on the table. I see this as an opportunity to talk to her about her feelings. I tell her she looks really frustrated, and I listen as she tells me why. Together we talk about different tools she can use to calm down and feel better. Maybe she could ask for help, take some deep breaths, or walk away for a few minutes. This discussion helps her identify what she is feeling and it teaches her how to deal with the experience.

Identifying feelings

My daughter is only three so she often needs help identifying her feelings. Young children may have a hard time identifying and discussing emotions because the words have not yet entered their vocabulary. A feelings poster in your child's room or somewhere in your house is an easy way to identify emotions. It contains many different faces with the emotions listed underneath. If your children are unable to give you a word to describe how they are feeling, they can just point to a face. One of my clients had her children practice different "feelings faces" in the mirror. Once they identified what each face represented, she took pictures of them and created a personalized "feelings sheet" with their photos.

Expressing feelings through behavior

I suggest to my clients that they talk to their children about feelings after a behavior episode (hitting, tantrums, or inappropriate language). Inappropriate behavior often signals that your child is dealing with a strong emotion and he or she is not sure how to deal with it. Hitting and other types of aggression often result from an inability to communicate feelings or feeling misunderstood. Discipline is usually necessary after a child demonstrates aggression, but I recommend a follow up discussion as part of the routine. The follow-up discussion after discipline provides an opportunity to discuss why the behavior was inappropriate and what can be done differently next time. It's an opportunity to teach *and* an opportunity for your child to be heard. This concept is an important teaching tool for younger children, and it can lead to increased communication with older children.

A father in one of my classes was heartbroken and frustrated when his oldest daughter yelled, "I hate you!" after a disagreement. Feeling empowered to talk about feelings, he went home that night and told her that it is okay to feel anger and frustration but it is not okay for her to use hurtful words and a disrespectful tone. They calmly discussed what she could do next time she felt strong emotion. He told me it was the longest discussion he ever had with this teenage daughter, and he felt they were creating a new way to communicate.

Role modeling feelings

Having an emotional experience in front of a child is often unavoidable. If you are frustrated or sad, it is okay to show how you are feeling—especially if you discuss what you are going to do to help yourself feel better. Witnessing a parent dealing with emotions can be a valuable learning experience for your children—they are able to watch the release and the recovery.

Demonstrating emotion can be educational, but seeking comfort from your child is not appropriate. The parent is the caregiver in the relationship and children should never feel it is their responsibility to console or take care of you. Through role modeling you give permission to show and discuss feelings in a safe environment. For example, one of my clients was devastated when the family pet died. She tried to hold it together and be strong "for her kids," but she noticed that her sons were beginning to shut down and spend a lot of time alone. During a family dinner my client could no longer handle what she was feeling and she began to cry. Her sons and husband began to cry along with her. They spent the rest of the evening discussing their loss and how good it felt to grieve together.

When children share

When children decide to share how they feel with you, it is important to validate what they are experiencing. If they tell you they are scared of the dark, they are looking for understanding and support. Telling them that they should not be scared or that they are too old to be afraid is not respectful of their inner experience, and it may result in a communication shutdown. Ask what scares them and ask what you can do to help.

My daughter recently told me she is afraid of her reflection in the window. We had a big discussion about a window reflection being just like a mirror. We also talked about how she could make funny faces at herself to make it less scary. When I asked what I could do to help her she said, "Just close the blinds." Sometimes it's that simple!

The Importance of Self Care

If I could send just one message to parents it would be the importance of self care. I wrote this article after reading Cheryl Richardson's book, Take Time for Your Life. She explains that extreme self care is about caring for ourselves so we have the ability to care for others. We need to practice self love and find our own happiness instead of looking for it outside of ourselves.

Understanding this concept and practicing it are two different things. When two of my daughters were babies I refused to hire a babysitter because I was uncomfortable being away from them. One day I had something that resembled a breakdown on the kitchen floor, and my husband insisted that we find someone to help us with childcare. Once a week for three hours a wonderful young girl would come over and play with my daughters. They loved her and I loved those three hours. I began to appreciate that taking care of yourself is an essential part of effective parenting.

Lesson: *It's time to let go of martyrdom. Ask for help and accept help when it is offered. Instead of talking to your children about self love and self fulfillment, role model what it means.*

୭ଡ଼

Take care of yourself. I respect and understand that your life is busy, unpredictable, and often challenging, but I recommend that you add self care to your agenda. It may seem paradoxical, but the reality is that if you take care of yourself, you can become a better caregiver.

I often hear from clients that they are "losing themselves" to parenthood or that their life is becoming a blur. This is a choice and not an absolute. You lose yourself to parenthood when you put everyone's needs in front of your own. Your life becomes a blur when you don't take time to think, plan, learn, or be thankful. If you are giving away your time, energy, and love on a consistent basis without taking time to refuel, you will naturally become drained.

Self care is personal; it means something different to everybody. One of my clients desires thirty minutes of alone time in the morning, while another needs her morning jog. Other clients need time with friends, weekly dates with significant others, or time to be creative. One of my clients decided she wanted to go back to graduate school and figured out that she could do this online. One of my friends realized that she missed watching live music, so she made a goal to see a live band at least once a month. She even keeps a CD of live music in her car just as a reminder.

Take a few minutes to figure how you can best take care of yourself.

- What gives me energy?
- Who gives me energy?
- When do I feel calm and centered?
- When do I feel fulfilled?
- How can I use my talents and my skills?
- How can I become more conscious so I can appreciate the gifts in my life?

As a parent you have a different reality—you may not be able to do everything you want whenever you want to do it. The goal is to figure out how to incorporate what you desire into your existing situation.

- How can I incorporate these things into my life?
- How can I be realistic about these expectations?
- What do I want my life to look and feel like?
- Who will support me? Who will help me?

Have a vision in place so you know where you are headed. Finding a support network is not only important for implementation, but also for keeping you on track. You need people who will help with obvious issues like babysitting, and you also need people who support your goal to take care of yourself.

Once you take action and implement your plan, become aware of how you feel when you make yourself a priority. Understand that your individual shift will make an impact on a larger scale. Are your children seeing you smile more? Are you kinder to your significant other? Do you have a better relationship with your friends? Notice how taking care of yourself can actually benefit the people around you.

Think of self care as a valuable lesson for your children. You are demonstrating the importance of having personal interests and an inner life. You are increasing your ability to be tuned into their needs, and you are bringing contentment into the home.

One of my many self-care goals is to spend special time with my girlfriends at least once a month. When this day rolls around, I make a point to tell my daughters how excited I am to spend time with my friends. I tell them the names of all of my friends, and sometimes I show them pictures. This usually initiates a wonderful conversation about my daughter's friendships and recent play dates. My daughters hang out with me while I get dressed and we listen to music. As I leave the house, they give me a hug (usually with very few tears) and they wave to me with a smile. My hope is that these experiences teach them the importance of friendship and having fun, and that mommy will have even more energy and love to share when she returns.

Misbehavior and Discipline

After working with lots of different families, I realized that many parents are easily offended by their children. They view their children's negative behavior as some sort of personal slight, and I wrote this to share a different perspective on misbehavior and discipline.

Know that children are supposed to test limits. They are attempting to learn boundaries because they came into the world without societal rules. As parents we are their first, and most important, teachers.

Lesson: *Take the time to realize your values and set your expectations so you know what you want to teach your children. Seek ways to be proactive rather than constantly reactive to their behavior. Give yourself, and your children, the gift of clarity.*

᙮

Children misbehave. They do not come to us civilized. Children need to learn, and parents are educators. The word discipline does not mean to punish, to ostracize, or cut down. "Discipline" comes from the word "disciple," which means "to teach." Children try to figure out their boundaries and limits at each developmental level. A parental goal is to understand the developmental level of children to better comprehend why they try certain things (they throw their cup on the floor because they are learning about gravity or cause and effect) and what we can teach them (if you throw your cup, you clean up the mess). Do not take misbehavior personally. Instead, begin to understand and respect your child's learning process.

One of my clients has a three-year-old daughter who struggles with sharing. This is a typical developmental issue for a three year old, and it is also a valuable teaching opportunity. When she witnessed her child not sharing, her usual response was to take the toy out of her daughter's hand and just give it to the other child, or she would yell at her daughter and then apologize to everyone because as a parent, she felt embarrassment.

After learning more about her daughter's developmental level, she realized this behavior was normal and that it presented an opportunity to discuss solutions. This is what many refer to as "the teachable moment."

The next time her daughter struggled with sharing, Mom got down to her daughter's level (instead of talking down to her) and asked her if she had any suggestions to solve this problem. Her daughter responded, "I want this crayon, she can find a different one." Mom acknowledged this solution but attempted to offer more socially conscious approaches: she suggested that her daughter could choose a different crayon, let her friend use the crayon first, play with something else for a little while, or walk away for a minute and think about it. Mom found that if she approached the situation calmly with the intent to teach, a solution was usually found and, in turn, her daughter learned a problem-solving technique.

Aggression or out of control behavior

If children are hitting, kicking, or simply out of control, they may be acting out of frustration or an inability to communicate. Most young children will try hitting or kicking. It is an impulsive choice and unfortunately, some find it effective. Think about the long-term effect of choosing aggression as a coping tool. Understand the importance of consistency and clarity when you are dealing with aggressive behavior from children. Time out can be used for aggression if framed appropriately. A client had a five-year-old son who frequently became aggressive. Sometimes she gave him a time out, and sometimes she didn't. She was not sending a clear message. Mom decided to make a commitment to be consistent with the time out approach. She told her son that if he hits, this tells her that he needs time away from others to calm down. If her son was really out of control, she sometimes had to sit with him and calmly hold him to keep him safe. After he completed the time out, she talked to him about what he did (you hit), why it was wrong (hitting hurts and we do not allow hitting in this family), and what he could do next time (use your words if you are frustrated, ask for help, walk away). She also prompted her son to apologize to the person he hit because hitting is not a way to solve problems. Mom was consistent with this process and eventually her son abandoned aggression and demonstrated the ability to use more appropriate coping tools.

The problem with "no"

Parents often find themselves saying "no" several times a day. Unfortunately, when you say no to children, they often get suited up for a battle or at the very least ask a lot of questions that start with "Why?" Consider reframing your response to a question. For example, your child wants a cookie. Instead of just saying no, you could say, "We are not going to have a cookie right now, but we will be having dinner soon. You will love dinner tonight." Your child is getting an answer to his question without the shutdown of a "no."

This response also moves the discussion into another topic and it may eliminate the need for the "why" questions. If your child wants you to buy a toy at the store, instead of just saying no, you could say, "Wow, that is a great toy. We are not going to buy it today, but I understand why you like it. Let's think about some of the toys you have at home. I really love your toy boat." Again, you eliminate the no, but you validate her desire and you continue to focus on her interests. A woman in one of my classes was frustrated because she loved to listen to talk radio in the car, but her daughter always asked to listen to music. My client's usual response was no, and this often resulted in an argument that caused them to stop talking the rest of the way home. Mom began to reframe her response by saying, "We are not going to listen to music now, but when we get home you can use the CD player and listen to your music," or, even better, "Why don't we split up the time? Do you want to listen to your music on the way there, or on the way home?" She offered her daughter a choice and she also demonstrated the value of sharing.

In charge or in control?

Understand that as a parent you are in charge. This is different than being in control. If you try to control, it will often result in a power struggle. Who can yell louder? Who can hold out the longest? This is an endless game and it does not teach healthy skills for adulthood. Respect your child as a person with an opinion and allow for the freedom of choice. For example, I like it when my daughter has her hair out of her face, so I prefer putting her hair in a ponytail. She likes to wear her hair down. I have realized over time that this topic leads to a power struggle between us and this is not a battle that needs to be fought (hairdo choice is not an important adult skill!). Now, when hair time rolls around, I ask her if she wants a ponytail or a barrette to keep her hair back. Her eyes light up and she puts her finger to her mouth so she can think carefully about the decision. We talk through her plans for the day so she can make an informed choice. Most days she wants to wear one of her colorful barrettes, but every once in awhile, she smiles at me and asks for a ponytail.

If your daughter struggles with getting dressed in the morning, get out a few outfits and let her pick which one she wants to wear (with young children, try to limit the choice to no more than two items). If it is time to get out of the bath and your son is not ready, ask him if he needs one more minute or two more minutes. If your children are arguing or not sharing, tell them they have a choice—they can play together nicely, or they can play separately. Giving them ownership over these situations can eliminate power struggles, and it also teaches them to use their problem-solving skills. As a parent you are still in charge, but you allow your children to play a role in the process.

The Joy of Learning

When I worked at Children's Memorial Hospital in Chicago I spent a great deal of time helping parents navigate the educational system. I found that many parents were unsure of how to support their children in school, and they often went to extremes. They were either completely disconnected or overly involved, which sometimes resulted in conflict. This was written to encourage learning at home while partnering with the teachers at school.

I also wanted parents to question how they view education and what they really want for their children. The school system is set up so test scores become the greatest indicator of success, but in reality, this is not true. Real success is about enjoying the learning process, finding teachers that inspire you, and discovering your real gifts so you can share them with the world. Grades and test scores have their purpose, but don't allow them to be the only indicator of your child's potential.

Lesson: *The most successful leaders and the most influential people are not always great test takers. Instead, they are curious, creative, and they think without boundaries. Innovators know their interests and they believe in themselves and their ability to make a difference. Inspire your children to follow their own path, trust their instincts, and discover the joy in learning.*

∽

Success in education is now defined as a respectable score on a standardized test. Lack of funding and the focus on testing has also led to a significant cut in creative programs, such as art and music. Social and artistic programs inspire imagination and creativity so children can see the possibilities within themselves, yet these programs are becoming nonexistent. I am afraid that the legacy for our children will be a learning environment based on memorization and regurgitation. It will be a challenge to sustain the joy of learning if this is the case.

Parents can play a positive role in this process by contributing to and supporting their children's natural desire to learn. Parents can focus on important parts of the child that the standardized tests miss: artistic ability, emotional awareness, creativity, and imagination. Parents can help their children find the joy in learning so they are motivated to find their passion and become lifelong learners.

Discover their interests, share your interests

Consistently discover and uncover the possibilities in your children. What makes them feel alive? When are they alert and aware? When do they ask questions? *Notice these experiences and let them know you are interested.* When you discover your children's interests you can support their growth.

- Help them check out books about a topic of interest.
- Tape an educational show about an interesting subject that you can watch together.
- Talk to them in real-world examples about how school subjects or interests can benefit them in the future (i.e., if they love poetry tell them it can help with writing music. If they struggle with math, demonstrate how math is used in the real world).
- Talk to your children about their dreams for the future. Let them know you are excited about who they are and who they can become.

Share your interests with your children. Show them that learning and growing still plays a role in your life. It can be your work, your volunteer experiences, your hobbies, or just fun activities.

- Take them to community dance programs, art museums, and libraries.
- Take them to a place where they can hear live music.
- Read with your children and read in front of your children on a daily basis.
- Provide an optimistic viewpoint of their future so they are free to imagine the possibilities.

Focus on their creativity

Support children in discovering their creativity. Provide experiences where they can be imaginative.

- Turn off the television and other screen technology and encourage your kids to be active and social.
- Have artistic tools available so they can draw and paint.
- Encourage journal writing.
- Buy an inexpensive CD player just for your children so they can listen to music and dance whenever they desire.

One of my clients was always frustrated that her children complained of being bored. I like to reframe this word so parents begin to look at boredom as an opportunity for their child. Parents usually have a bad reaction to this word because they feel obligated to entertain their child, but in actuality this is an opportunity for the child to be imaginative and creative. Next time your children tell you they are bored, surprise them by saying, "Wonderful! Now you have the opportunity to be creative. I can't wait to see what you do."

Support your children's school experience

Understand the effect of your words. Talk about your children's school with excitement and respect.

- Talk about homework as an opportunity to learn and grow, not as if it were a punishment.
- Talk about teachers and school staff in a respectful manner in front of your children. If you are speaking poorly about authority figures in front of your children, they may feel that they have permission to be disrespectful as well.
- Be available at some point during their homework time. Even if they don't need help, you can show interest in what they are doing and provide praise and encouragement.

Teachers have the daunting task of being educators, social workers, and disciplinarians to a large classroom of children. Even the most dedicated teacher cannot spend individual time with each student every day.

Teachers need parents to process daily classroom activities with their children and encourage and support the learning process.

Finally, support your children as they learn by creating a calm and quiet place to study at home.

- Make sure their study place has all the necessary tools for learning (pencils, paper, calculator).
- Make sure their study place is well lit without obvious distractions (research has shown that classical music can aid in the learning process, but television can negatively affect focus and attention).
- Assist them with organizational skills so they know when assignments are due.

One of my clients has a big family calendar on the wall so it is clear when her children have a test or an assignment due. Another client made a checklist so her children remember what they need to bring to school and what they need to bring home. Teachers are often willing to initial these checklists so parents know that homework assignments are written down correctly. Help your children develop a sense of control over their educational expectations so they can focus their energy on learning.

The Family Meal

I don't enjoy cooking. When my husband suggested that we have a family meal, I envisioned myself miserable at the stove. I finally agreed to make this a priority and learned that the family meal is not about food, it's about what happens around the table.

Our family meal has become a time to communicate and practice awareness. When we sit down to eat we join hands and take a big deep breath. This helps us let go of where we were and focus on where we are. Then each of us shares what we are grateful for and we send positive thoughts to anyone who is sick or needs support. It's our special time for presence and gratitude.

Lesson: *The family meal is not just about eating, it's about setting aside time to slow down, communicate, and reconnect with each other.*

❧

I remember the day my husband told me he wanted our family to eat together at least once a day. I believed we were already eating several meals together. We always seemed to be in the kitchen at the same time in the morning, and we were usually all present in the house for dinner. He adjusted his request by specifying that he wanted us to *sit down at the same table together* for at least one meal.

My initial reaction was panic because I envisioned cooking, placemats, and lots of cleanup. I have never thought of myself as a cook. I am not one of those people who claim to be "relaxed" by cooking. Instead, cooking conjures up memories of several failed attempts at baking homemade cakes when I was little and the anxiety I feel when someone suggests I "bring a dish" to a party.

I make a point to feed my children healthy food, but the choices are usually served separately—a piece of cheese, some turkey, a carrot, and some blueberries—not very exciting. Deciding on a main dish and mixing items together to actually create a meal is not typical in my house.

The first night we decided to try this new approach to family togetherness, we kept it simple. My husband grilled fish, and I made a salad (salad in a bag!) and boiled some pasta. We sat down at the table and I watched in amazement as Jacey ate salmon as if it was a McDonald's cheeseburger and Camryn ate wheat pasta and salad. This was too easy. I realized that my failed attempts at cake baking had put some serious roadblocks in my mind when it came to anything in the kitchen.

Jacey wanted to get up from the table several times to do a dance, which prompted a natural time to discuss table manners. Not only could we discuss etiquette, but we could do this without the noise of everyday life. The radio was off, there was no television in sight, and the phone was not answered. We spoke sentences to each other instead of sound bites. I immediately understood that eating together provided a chance to slow down, look at each other, and talk. I teach classes on effective family communication, and now I understand that people need more than communication tools—they need the daily opportunity to use them.

The next morning I decided to replace the word "cooking" with "preparing." I prepare a wonderful salad, I prepare pasta perfectly, and I know exactly how long to prepare fresh corn in the microwave. Now when life gets busy or we don't feel like "preparing," we might decide to purchase a meal and bring it home, but we still sit down at that table. I am thankful to my husband for suggesting that we eat together on a daily basis, and I am proud of myself for realizing that I do have some skills that help feed my family. Who knows, maybe I should give that cake another try.

Freedom to Be

This was written when my oldest daughter was in preschool and she was very quiet. At home she talked, but in public situations she would often refuse to speak. Initially my husband and I struggled with her silence and we searched for the boundary between teaching manners and allowing her to "be."

We offered suggestions and we modeled appropriate behavior. At times we felt frustration and embarrassment when she refused to speak, but we also understood that she was very young. We trusted that at some point she would find her voice.

We found that the more we let go, the more she opened up. My daughter's communication skills have developed and not by our insistence—it was her natural progression. It has been a welcome surprise when she offers a "hello" or "thank you" to a teacher or neighbor. It has been a joy to watch her interact on play dates and at swimming classes, when just a year ago she had no interest. It feels good because I know she is intrinsically motivated. She is not saying hello because she is trying to avoid punishment, and she isn't going to a friend's house because we are forcing her to do so. She is doing it because she is ready.

Lesson: *Sometimes you have to have the end in mind when teaching your children. Do you want them to do something simply to please you, or do you give them enough space and time to find what pleases them? You have to consider safety and boundaries, but when it's simply about readiness and interests, allow your children to take the lead. Instead of focusing on who you want them to be, let them tell you who they are.*

I recently took Jacey to a birthday party and the invitation said to wear a tutu. She decided to wear her butterfly wings instead. When we got to the party she quietly watched as the other girls ran around and chased each other in their tutus. She decided to sit a few seats away when the group began to work on art projects. I watched my daughter and wondered if she wished she had a tutu, if she wanted to go home, or if she somehow needed my support.

Just before cake she told me that she needed to go to the bathroom. Once we closed the door in the bathroom she started to jump up and down and told me what a great time she was having. She started naming off all of the little girls in the room and telling me how her whole class was there. Much to my surprise, she was having a wonderful time. As we returned to the room she gathered with the other girls to look at the candles on the cake. For the last thirty minutes of the party she was running, laughing, and enjoying the experience.

Freedom to choose

Giving your children space to make their own decisions can be challenging and sometimes uncomfortable. I try to focus on what I really want for my daughter—to trust her own instincts and do what feels right for her. I could have told her that she should wear a tutu like all the other girls at the party. I also could have pushed her into interacting with the other children as soon as we got there by saying something like: "All the other kids are playing, why don't you?" I could have asked her what was wrong or asked her why she was being so shy. I have been tempted to do all of these things, but I know it would not be in her best interest. It would have been for my social comfort rather than her benefit.

Freedom to feel

Children feel safe when they feel heard and respected. Sometimes they still have to do what they don't want to do, but provide an opportunity to express their feelings and receive support and reassurance. For example, if your children fall down and feel pain, allow them to cry and feel the pain instead of continuously telling them they are okay or that it wasn't that bad. Sometimes they will cry harder to show you that it really did hurt. Give them language for their pain (that looked like it hurt, or ouch) rather than telling them they don't actually feel it. Sometimes a reassuring smile or hug is all they need while they cry their pain away.

If your children express fear or nervousness, allow them to talk about these feelings and respect what they are telling you. I once worked with a father who decided to dunk his son's head under water even after his son expressed fear of being submerged. The son became quite upset and eventually lost interest in swimming. The father thought he was being helpful because *he* didn't think his son should be afraid. Instead of listening to his son he made a decision based on his experiences as an adult.

Freedom within limits

Healthy parenting also includes structure, discipline, and respect for parental authority. Rules designed for safety and appropriate social behavior are a necessary part of functioning in the world.

There is a difference between following rules and asserting self-expression. If you tell your children something that they don't want to hear, like finish your chores or time for bed, they may get upset. Let them know that you hear their frustration. This doesn't mean that they don't have to do what you asked, but give them the satisfaction of knowing their feelings are heard. Saying, "I hear that you don't want to pick up your toys, but we have to clean up before we do anything else," can be so much more effective than a lecture about how you clean the house and pick up their things every day.

My daughter often cries when I tell her it's time to clean up and go to bed. I have tried talking to her about bed time, waking up early, and all the other reasons she needs sleep, but the most effective approach to helping her calm down is being with her in the moment. In a calm voice I tell her that I hear and see her disappointment, but it is still time to go to bed. This usually leads to a hug and a calm discussion about everything she has to look forward to in the morning. Simple acknowledgment can often eliminate a power struggle or an escalation to frustration.

Freedom to find interests

When children find a healthy interest, it's important to support their choice. Their interests may be different than yours and this can be challenging for many parents. Maybe you envisioned watching your daughter at a ballet recital, but she shows more interest in softball. Maybe you envisioned coaching your son's baseball team, but he shows more interest in his piano lessons. Maybe you are an outgoing, talkative person but your child prefers small groups and alone time. You can share who you are and your interests with your children, but leave room for their own passions and true character to emerge.

When children are young we tend to push them to do what their peers are doing. Yet as children get older, we hope they trust their own instincts rather than do whatever their peers are doing. Their confusion should be no surprise. Children have their own unique way of dealing with the world, and as parents it is our job to realize who they are and support them the best we can. Giving children permission to be themselves establishes self worth and leads to a life of limitless possibilities.

The Miscarriage

This was written two days after I miscarried my third child. This essay was not initially written for publication, it was more of a therapeutic exercise to release this overwhelming experience.

I decided to include it in this book because, unfortunately, miscarriages are common. A miscarriage is an experience that necessitates processing and healing, yet our culture often urges us to move on and just "try again."

Lesson: *This might be helpful for a husband/partner to understand what a woman can experience when she miscarries. My husband was saddened and disappointed by our loss, but even with his empathetic nature he was challenged to understand how painful this was for me. He wanted to help, but I was often unable to express what I needed. Through trial and error he learned that he did not need to say the perfect words or buy me the perfect thing; he just needed to allow me to grieve. He often had to sit in the discomfort of my unhappiness, which is not an easy thing to do. At night he would rub my feet or just lie down with me while I rested or stared blankly at a television. His presence and understanding were the best gift, and really the only gift, he could give me.*

∽

For some reason I took the girls to my appointment. I have had many doctor appointments over the years, but I had never thought to bring the girls. I guess I thought I should be alone or just with my husband "just in case" something was wrong. But this was my third pregnancy, and I had seen this baby's heartbeat. I had spent over a year and half deciding whether or not our family was ready for this child. For some, the number of children they have is a simple decision, but I was unsure. I was full of fear, and either possibility had a tendency to make me dizzy. I came from a family of two. My sister had a family of two. How could I handle a family of three? At the same time I felt a longing, a need to process through these emotions and reach a well thought out decision because I felt there was something important and meaningful on the other side. After counseling, praying, and much needed silence, I realized that someone was missing from this family. Making the decision was exciting and liberating because I broke through patterns and cleared out useless fear. I was ready to move forward.

The doctor comes in, says hi to the girls, and passively asks how I feel. I proudly report that although I had been desperately sick from weeks six to ten, my symptoms have magically disappeared. In my mind I attribute this to a few acupuncture appointments and a necessary attitude adjustment. I made myself better. I can tell the doctor does not like this news, and she asks if I have any other pregnancy symptoms. My heart goes to my throat—I sense concern. I have never had a bad doctor appointment. I have never seen this look. Things begin to move in slow motion as she reaches for the Doppler to locate my baby's heartbeat. She moves it around my stomach. I realize she cannot find it. As if in a dream, I sit up and slowly say, "You can't find it, can you." Interestingly, my girls are quiet and calm—they can feel the tension in the air. Next thing I know I am heading to the hospital for an ultrasound and trying to find my sister to watch the kids. Unfortunately, I am going to have this experience alone because my husband is driving home from an out of town work trip.

I'm driving to the hospital and my husband continues to reassure me over the phone that everything is fine. He tells me this ultrasound will be a validation that our baby is healthy. The doctor *had* said that sometimes eleven weeks is too early to pick up a heartbeat on a Doppler. My intuitive abilities are gone. I don't know what to believe. I have tackled too much for this pregnancy not to progress. The process of deciding whether or not to have this child had been a spiritual awakening, a new chapter of my adult life. This child is supposed to come.

As I lie down for my ultrasound, the technician kindly holds my head and tells me to hope for the best. I watch her face rather than the screen. I see her shake her head, and I realize the news is not good. I slowly look over at the screen and I see my very little baby. I can tell this child is not alive. There is no movement, no signs of health. The baby on the screen will be always be etched in my mind. I let out a loud sound as if I had just been hit. I have never felt such emotion. I cannot hold my baby, kiss it, or soothe it. I vaguely remember the technician saying that the baby only measured at nine weeks. In my case, ending morning sickness early was an indication that this pregnancy had come to an end.

My sadness is painful and profound. Every doctor and nurse tell me this is not my fault, but I look back and wonder what I could have done differently. I am astounded at the number of people that tell me they suffered a miscarriage—family members, close friends, and the surgical nurse who held my hand through the D&C. This is an ache I have never known. Women can create life; but when the life does not sustain, there is a deep, eternal pain. What do I do next? I'm not sure, but I am thankful that women chose to share their stories of survival with me.

I know I am already blessed with two children. I am lucky to have my daughters, and now when I look at them I realize this more than I did before. People have told me it is worse to miscarry a first pregnancy because there is a greater hopelessness. This may be true, but it doesn't alleviate my sadness.

This is my experience, and I have to accept it. I will sharpen up my spiritual understanding so I can find a place to put it. I hope to hold onto my optimism so when ready, we might undergo the process again. I know there are things for me to learn and this baby was one of my teachers. This baby was my child, and while he or she was alive I was as happy as I have ever been. I explain to my daughters that the baby we love and talk so much about has stopped growing and will not be coming. My three year old hugs my stomach and quietly asks, *"Maybe another baby will come?"* With hope but undeniable uncertainty I can only answer, *"Maybe."*

Yoga Gratitude

The intention of this article was to share the importance of yoga in my life and the value of being present with my children. But now, in hindsight, I think I was still trying to process my miscarriage. I craved normalcy, and I was having trouble staying in the moment.

Lesson: *Yoga is the great teacher of being present, breathing through tension and uncertainty, and finding space within the discomfort. Yoga is a physical practice, but the same principles can be applied to our emotional experiences.*

∾

During a yoga class I attempt to move into a challenging position called pigeon. As I struggle to move my leg into the correct place, my instructor explains that wherever I am is exactly where I am supposed to be. She says there are benefits to where I am now and this is what I need to appreciate. I hear her words, but I still push myself to get my leg flat on the floor. I want to get there *now*.

I acknowledge that I struggle with appreciating the moment. Sometimes I just want to know what will happen and where I should be instead of experiencing the journey. My whole life I have searched for meaning; but instead of accepting where I am, I realize I am often searching for signs that it will all be okay. I know that's not how it works. Real life is venturing into the unknown. There is no way to know that everything will be okay and nor should there be. I can look at all the challenging experiences in my life and realize their importance in the person I have become. I understand this but I often have a hard time letting go and being "here."

As a parent I am often challenged to stay in the moment with my girls. Instead of appreciating that my daughter is soothed by her pacifier, I tend to focus my attention on the dentist who warned me about "orthodontic issues" later in life. Instead of accepting that right now my daughters are afraid of monsters, I worry that they will always be fearful at bedtime.

I know this is common because my clients have similar worries. Some parents worry incessantly that their infants' unpredictable sleeping patterns will continue into the teenage years, or they are already concerned that their two year old will be bullied when he heads off for school. I share with them the same thing I say to myself: The more we stay focused on today, the less we have to worry about the future. If we react to our children based on our fear of what they will become, we cannot truly appreciate who they are right now. Children are in the moment, and we need to be there with them.

Jacey was recently allowed to see a movie where the antagonist character had questionable values. She has become intrigued with this character and she spends time pretending to be him. My first thought (or fear) is that this is not okay. Why does she want to be this character? Will she emulate his behavior? Fortunately, my professional instincts eventually kick in and I realize that she is exploring a different side of herself. She is trying out what she has seen to see how it fits. By staying in the moment with her, I realize she is right where she needs to be. She is discovering different choices and parts of the human experience. This is an important part of her self-discovery.

Camryn just turned two and I notice the differences between her and Jacey. I get concerned when I realize she doesn't have as many words or as much desire to play alone, but at the same time I recognize her maturity and social skills seem stronger. Although stopping all of this endless processing is a challenge, I can recognize that it is irrelevant. I want to stand back so I can let her become who she is supposed to be without my futile concern. My concern about what skill she should or shouldn't have right now does not serve her. My real desire is to let her know that *I believe in the person she is today* and I will always be here to support her along her journey.

My yoga teacher offers cues to help me ease into pigeon position and she reminds me to breathe and have faith that everything is unfolding as it should. As I look around the room, I realize I am not alone; others are struggling with the pose. I decide to breathe and let my leg be where it wants to be. I feel a wonderful stretch in my hip—a place that really needed to be stretched. I realize this is what my body needs right now. I can appreciate that I am not ready to be in full pigeon pose. I guess this is where I am supposed to be.

Focus on the Strengths

Clients and students usually seek my services because they are worried about their children and they want to share their concerns. After listening intently I usually say, "Tell me what they do well." This can be jarring and sometimes they need a minute or two to come up with a list of strengths. Parents spend too much energy on worry and what might go wrong. Children do great things every day and they need someone to notice.

__Lesson:__ Issues need to be addressed and challenges need to be dealt with, but pay just as much attention to what is working. Part of your job as a parent is to notice your children's skills and potential. If you don't, who will?

᎒᎓

Recently I sat with a group of parents as we watched our children take swimming lessons. While our kids splashed around in the water, the parents all talked about the actions and abilities of the children in the pool.

"My daughter is not a good swimmer."
"My son needs to kick his legs harder, he's not even moving!"
"Look at my daughter, she never pays attention."
"My son is such a baby, he hates to go underwater."

I didn't hear any comments about how much fun the kids were having or how their skills were developing. The parents had decided to focus their attention on the difficulties rather than the successes.

Parents often set their sights on fixing what is "broken" rather than witnessing the joy in the present moment. If we constantly put our attention on things that bother us, we are going to see more things that bother us. If we begin to focus our attention on strengths and cherish the moments, we will have more moments to cherish.

One of my favorite parts about being a parent coach is helping parents focus on the positive attributes of their children. This doesn't mean that the challenging parts don't exist. It simply means that if more thought and energy is put toward the things we appreciate and love, these parts will ultimately grow and expand.

Focusing on strengths is very different than parental bragging or the "my child is the best" mentality. Comparing your children to other children will not create a healthy sense of self. They will not feel worthy in their accomplishments unless they are better than everybody else. Balanced statements such as, "I can tell you are working hard today," or "It looks like you are really enjoying this activity," are supportive and loving. These statements also demonstrate that you are intently watching and noticing their effort.

If you are unsure of your children's strengths, spend more time with them. Question them about their interests. When they are actively engaged in play, ask if you can join them. Make family time a priority rather than signing up for ten activities or five play dates a week. When you are on a walk, at the park, or at a sporting event turn your cell phone off so you can watch and participate with your child while they play. Take the time to notice this person growing and developing in front of you.

A parent has the opportunity to be their children's greatest advocate, and parenting is much more fun when energy is focused on what is working. Support your children through the challenges, help them navigate the difficult days, and make it a priority to recognize and point out their potential.

Without Limitations

I already had two children, but when I was expecting my third daughter I decided to investigate natural childbirth. I enlisted the help of a midwife, a doula, and a Bradley instructor and read books by Ina May Gaskin. I experienced a dramatic shift in perception—a new understanding of what women can do and a new appreciation for the importance of the birth process. This was written because as a woman I feel it's an important story to pass on.

Lesson: If you are interested in learning more about natural birth, don't wait until labor day. Begin the education process early in your pregnancy. Prepare your body and mind and enlist the support of educators and professionals. You will learn a great deal about the amazing miracle of birth, and you will also learn a great deal about yourself.

❧

After experiencing paralyzing ambivalence, I finally decided to have another baby. For a long time I was fearful and stuck, unsure of what was right for my family. Could I handle a bigger family? Was I willing to have a baby after thirty-five? Was I ready to go through morning sickness, pregnancy, and nursing again? After a great deal of soul searching I decided to take a step into the unknown. I knew this pregnancy and this birth would be different.

I wanted to eliminate unnecessary stress from this pregnancy. I gave away all of my pregnancy books that told me how bad I was going to feel and what to "watch out" for each month. I didn't want to live in fear this time. I decided to enjoy each moment of the experience. The books I chose described pregnancy as a time of joy and childbirth as a healthy, normal process. Rather than recommending that women avoid pain through medical intervention, they suggested becoming mentally and physically prepared for the labor experience. The books described natural birth as a rite of passage, a psycho-spiritual training ground for mother and child. They touted the health benefits to mother and baby and the bond that is formed during the birth process. This was something I wanted to experience.

Pregnancy and birth became my new adventure. My older daughters were born with the help of an epidural in a traditional hospital setting, but I decided that this time I wanted a place that supported a more natural experience. I found an Alternative Birthing Center and a midwife practice. I enlisted the help of a good friend who is a Bradley instructor and my parent coach, who also happens to be a birth doula. They taught me about the birth experience and provided me with tools to help with pregnancy and delivery. They helped me understand that though natural birth was the goal, I needed to be open to whatever might unfold. It's impossible to be in full control of pregnancy and birth. They helped me talk through my fear and they consistently empowered me. I surrounded myself with women who believed I could do this.

This adventure was not just for me, it was for my whole family. My husband became my birth partner, and my children experienced my monthly appointments with me. The midwives encouraged me to bring my daughters into the room so they could hear the heartbeat of their new sibling. Sometimes my girls would help by holding the Doppler or holding my hand. Almost nightly my husband and I talked about the pregnancy, our birth plan, and our expanding family.

As the months went by I became strong and confident. My body felt great and the traditional aches and pains were minor. My mind was stronger and my energy was better. I felt I was more effective as a mother, a partner, and as a coach. My boundaries were expanding, and I was open to taking more risks as a professional. I shared more of my writing, I made myself available for interviews, and I gave more presentations. My pregnancy experience was actually having a positive effect on my career.

As my due date drew near, I felt ready. I studied visualization and relaxation techniques. I was walking and doing yoga on a daily basis. It was like training for a marathon, and I felt prepared. But the due date came and went. I was initially frustrated but eventually amused by the continuing lessons coming my way. Patience and giving up control are essential lessons when you become a parent. My daughters had taught me this, and this baby was reminding me.

Eight days past my due date, I woke up to contractions. Believe it or not, I was excited to put all of my new tools to good use. I fully experienced the tremendous challenge of labor, but I continued to trust that the baby knew exactly what to do. As we drove to the birthing center in the middle of the night, running red lights, I lay on the floor of our minivan and realized the baby could not wait. I yelled to my husband to let him know I was about to give birth—I had no choice but to push. As we pulled up to emergency room, the baby's head was out. No one believed me and insisted that I sit in a wheelchair. I insisted that I needed to walk into the ER and immediately lay down, and a few seconds later my third daughter was born.

It was a whirlwind process, nothing I could have expected, but it was exactly the way it was supposed to be. I never expected or planned for a perfect birth. I just wanted to be present and participate. I felt open and prepared for whatever would unfold, and what came was a great story to tell for years to come.

I understand and respect that there are many ways to have a child. I am surrounded by loved ones that required medical intervention for pregnancy and labor, and I am humbled by the people and technology that helped their children come into the world. For me this journey was not just to experience natural birth, but to learn more about myself and what I am capable of doing. Women need to support each other and tell each other about the positive possibilities, not the possible negatives.

I am now more open and aware. This is one of the reasons we named our new little girl Skylar—she is a representation of expansiveness. I am excited to pass this learning experience on to all of my daughters. I feel a responsibility to raise my girls without limitations. I dedicate this journey to all of my children, but especially to my third child, a pregnancy I lost at eleven weeks. It was because of you that I decided to go deeper and discover a new path. Thank you for pointing out the direction I needed to go.

The Paci Party

This was my first published article based on a very memorable parenting experience. Like other parents I struggled with getting rid of the pacifier, but I was never comfortable with the cold turkey approach. It took a lot of discussion and negotiation to create this plan, and thankfully the outcome was positive. I realize now that I depended on that pacifier as much as my daughter and I was just as sad to let it go. My daughter was challenged to find new tools to calm herself, and I was challenged to find new tools to be an effective parent.

Lesson: When it is time for your children to make a big change, ask their opinion, get them involved, and move forward together.

☜

When my daughter was born she took to the pacifier immediately. It soothed her in every situation—restaurants, the middle of the night, between feedings, on an airplane. It was her solace, and we made sure we carried it everywhere we went.

As she grew up, her love affair with the paci (as she calls it) continued. The need for one paci grew to two—one for her mouth and one for her hand—just in case. The paci continued to soothe her when she fell or when she felt misunderstood. For her it was immediate comfort.

It was getting to that time when most children her age were giving up the pacifier, usually because the parents felt it was the right time. We had talks with my daughter about letting go of the pacifier, but with great conviction she told us she was not ready.

There were comments from caring friends who said "it only gets harder" if we allowed her to keep it. Others warned us about the "dangers" to her teeth. We knew this advice was given with good intentions, but we were not willing to take the pacifier away without my daughter having a role in the process. She used the pacifier to soothe her body and mind, and we didn't want this to come to an abrupt halt. We decided to do it slowly.

We started to put some boundaries around the pacifier—she was always welcome to use it, but she had to be in her room. Later we decided it was only to be used before nap or bedtime. She handled these subtle transitions with ease. She began to find different soothing techniques during the day, but at night she still looked forward to the comfort of the paci.

On her birthday we gave her a bag with four pacifiers. We explained that these would be the "final four." She was responsible for them, and she would decide when to give them up. Together we brainstormed four celebrations, one for each pacifier. For number one we would go to the library, for number two she could pick her favorite restaurant for dinner, and for number three she could buy a book at the bookstore. For number four we would plan a "paci party" with dinner, cake, and a movie.

She gave up the first pacifier immediately. She handed it over without a thought, and we headed out to the library. A week later the second pacifier was handed over, and we had a wonderful dinner that night full of toasts to her growth and new beginnings. The third pacifier was given up two days later, and she chose a princess book from the bookstore.

Then came the big lull—number four seemed to be staying put. A few times it got lost and we explained she would have to find it on her own. She had been told it was her responsibility, and we stuck by that decision. With great compassion we would tell her that maybe it knew it was time to go. She would begin to frantically search and, of course, that thing would always turn up. I think we thought the pacifier would eventually develop a hole or she would lose it, but she learned to put it in that bag every morning. It came out for an occasional cleaning, but otherwise it stayed safe.

My daughter held onto that one pacifier for a significant period of time. It was not always in her mouth at night—she held it a lot. She took responsibility for this paci, almost like a pet. We decided she needed some encouragement. We told her it was time to start planning the paci party and give up number four. We showed her a calendar, and she picked the date that felt right for her.

The day of the paci party we gave her a little pillow with her name on it. We sat together, and each member of the family hugged the pillow and "put our love into it" so she could have us with her while she slept.

Family members sent cards of encouragement and support that we read aloud. We had a wonderful night of celebration, and then it was time to go to bed. She lay on her bed with the paci in her mouth and I could see her brain churning. Since the day she came home from the hospital she has had this little piece of serenity, and it was time for her to say goodbye. She looked at me and put it in my hand. I hugged her and felt her shake. I backed up to wipe her tears and realized she was laughing. Her eyes were bright, and she was looking so proud and confident. We tucked her in with her new pillow and said goodnight, and she fell asleep with a smile on her face.

The only person who cried that night was me. As I threw that pink pacifier in the garbage, I thanked it for soothing my daughter and allowing her to go within and calm herself. I thanked it for all of the uninterrupted dinners at restaurants, all of the peaceful nights, and all of the plane rides when her ears were popping. I had a great appreciation for its role in my daughter's life, and I am glad she was able to let it go in such a positive way. It was her early childhood companion and now it was time to move on to new things. *Goodbye, old friend.*

True awareness and insight come when one is quiet and still. My daily experiences rarely have room for quiet, or at least I am often challenged to make it a priority. Watching my daughter Camryn take time for herself so naturally has become a helpful reminder. She is a happy little girl filled with love, compassion, and thoughtful ideas. I believe her connection to solitude contributes to her content nature, and I can only hope to follow her lead.

***Lesson:** Respect who your children are and see what they have to teach. Appreciate the importance of solitude and quiet — live it and allow for it.*

∾

My daughter Camryn reminds me of Ferdinand, the title character from the children's book by Munro Leaf. It is about a little bull that is expected to turn into a fierce fighting bull, but he prefers to sit under the big cork tree and smell the flowers. Mother Cow sometimes worries about Ferdinand because he always sits by himself under the tree. But when she checks on him to make sure he is not lonely, she realizes he is completely content in his stillness. She allows him to be who he is.

I want my child to be who she is, too. I think about Mother Cow when I find my daughter alone, deep in thought in the middle of a busy day. She will be active for awhile, but as soon as I can't find her I know exactly where she has gone. She is sitting in her room, most likely in her bed with all of her comforts—her books, animals, dolls, blankets. She might be reading a book, daydreaming, or otherwise lost in her thoughts.

She is different than her big sister. Jacey thrives on constant movement and activity. If she is not interacting with someone, she still experiences that person by closely observing his or her every move. She seems to derive energy from the outside world, an experience I can easily relate to.

Although I have yet to utter the words, "Why don't you get moving like your big sister?" the sentence has gone through my mind. When

I start to go into "compare" mode, I realize the person who needs the adjustment is not my daughter, it is me. When I start to feel unsettled because she is doing something she is perfectly content with, I realize it is time to take a breath and step back.

In reality, I appreciate that Camryn enjoys the quiet moments. She stays up late to enjoy the still and quiet house and she wakes up an hour after the rest of the family. Every morning she wants to sit on my lap and have a long hug. This is often a challenge when I am running around trying to get ready for the day. She enjoys the company of other children her age, but she doesn't seem upset when it is time for them to go. She has two invisible friends who travel with us when we go far from home. When we return home, she talks to them on the phone. She hands me the phone so I can tell them they are missed and let them know they are always welcome in our family. She smiles at people, and she is nice to the people she meets. Not by my insistence, but because it comes naturally.

Recently I signed her up for gymnastics, but after two weeks she decided she didn't like it. At first I was annoyed, frustrated at her lack of desire to participate, but she was calm when she told me, "No thank you, not right now." She seems to know her interests, and right now gymnastics is not one of them. She prefers talking to the trees, playing in the flowers, and watching the ants build their homes. The simple activities are her favorites.

At a very young age, my daughter seems to know how to take care of herself. And I not only need to allow it, I need to learn from it. Our fast-paced society can trick us into believing that constant activity and productivity are the only acceptable ways to live this life, and we fail to appreciate that finding balance can actually be healthier. We can enjoy interaction and activity, but we can also learn to appreciate the moment by finding stillness.

The other day I was feeling overwhelmed by my life and my list, just moving from one thing to the next without a great deal of thought. As I moved down the hallway, I could hear my daughter's quiet hums. I found her relaxing in her room with a big smile, so I lay down and gave her one of those long hugs she loves so much. I felt her joy and appreciated her as my teacher. I closed my eyes and pictured us together, underneath the big cork tree enjoying the smell of the flowers.

The Tantrum

This was written the same night as my daughter's tantrum. I realized that sometimes the best parenting decision is to stop and do nothing. Take a deep breath and acknowledge your feelings so you can deal with situation calmly and thoughtfully.

Lesson: Take care of your feelings of frustration before you deal with an important parenting decision. It's the best first step towards a positive outcome.

❦

She wants two books, not just one. I tell her that it is late and we have time for one book, but she insists on another. I tell her that she needs to pick the book quickly because it is almost time for bed. She doesn't want to pick just one book. She is frustrated, and her voice is getting louder. There is stomping, pleading, and then there are tears.

As soon as I hear the first wail, I know this might take awhile. Most of the time she can handle disappointment, but today is not one of those days. I know a good night's sleep will help, but she is unable to understand this. Right now she is having a tantrum.

My initial reaction is to recite every thought in my head: *"You know we only have time for one book." "You must be tired." "Why are you so upset?"* After a few minutes I realize she can't even hear my voice—she is crying too loud.

Then frustration kicks in. I think to myself: *You are too old to be crying like this. I need to get back to work. I don't have time for this. Maybe we won't read books at night anymore!* I think threatening thoughts because she seems out of control and it is making me uncomfortable. I want her to stop.

Her cries are loud and my threatening thoughts are about to come out of my mouth. I close my eyes and take a deep breath. I know this tantrum is an emotional release, and it is probably not about the book. It is probably about any number of things that happened during the day and the book was the last straw. She is tired, her tools are gone, and her emotions are on the surface. I think about earlier in the day when I was cleaning up the kitchen and trying to make lunch while feeling frustrated with my computer. She asked me a simple question and I promptly snapped back, "I can't deal with that right now. Can't you see that I am busy making lunch!" I did not cry at the top of my lungs, but I did overreact to something quite simple. So I can relate to what she is feeling right now.

I decide to pick her up and carry her to her bedroom. I put her in bed and sit on the floor. I say to her, "You are safe. I am here." I relax and I skim through one of her books. I do not talk to her or look at her; I am just there. I allow her to get whatever she is feeling out of her system, and I try to remain a calm presence in the room.

The cries seem to be slowing down—not quite as loud, not quite as frequent. I wait until I hear only sniffling and I look up at her. She is staring at me, not quite sure what just happened to her body. I ask her if she is feeling better and she nods. I ask her if she is ready to read a book now and she quietly says yes.

After the story I put the book down and ask her to tell me about what just happened, "What were you feeling, and how could I have helped you?" We talk about sadness and disappointment and how it feels inside of our body. We talk about how healthy it is to get it out, and we talk about other ways to release it. She says she likes to scribble pictures or roll around on the floor. I tell her that I like to go for a walk or talk to somebody that I love. Her eyes look exhausted, but she seems to feel heard and satisfied because she has a slight smile.

As I am leaving, she asks me if we can read two books tomorrow night. With a smile I tell her yes and I start to close her door. As I am about to walk away I hear a faint, "Thanks, Mama." It's amazing what one deep breath can do.

There's No Place Like Home

Watching The Wizard of Oz was a big event in our house. We planned, prepped, and anticipated, and when we watched we were completely present — no cell phones or computers allowed. The girls loved the movie, but they loved the uninterrupted family time even more.

Lesson: Children love to plan and experience family events, especially if they take an active role in the preparations. New traditions and family events create meaningful family memories.

∞

When I was a child I dressed up as Dorothy for Halloween three years in a row. I admit: *The Wizard of Oz* is my favorite movie. And although I consistently encourage parents not to push their hopes and dreams on their kids, deep down I was hoping my children would enjoy it.

This is a big movie that touches on a lot of different emotions, so we introduced it slowly. About a year ago I read them their first Wizard of Oz book, and we followed up with a thirty-minute Wizard of Oz cartoon that they still occasionally request. The books and cartoon made them familiar with the story, but I was most excited to introduce the soundtrack. I found a CD that has all of the songs from the movie and much of the movie dialogue as well. The girls played it over and over again on the CD player, until even I began to tire of "Somewhere Over the Rainbow."

After all of this preparation, we decided it was time to watch the "real" *Wizard of Oz.* As a family we looked at the calendar and we chose a Friday night. We had two weeks to think about it, talk about it, and get excited for it. We planned the menu, and we decided that we should wear our pajamas. In an effort to lessen potential fear, we decided to show the girls *The Wizard of Oz* movie trailer (which can be easily accessed on the Internet), so they could experience the wicked witch and the flying monkeys before the big event.

At night in their bunk beds the girls would ask, "Is it tomorrow? Is tomorrow the day?" And every morning the girls would ask me to count down the days on the calendar.

The day finally arrived, and we were all excited. It was like watching the movie for the first time (even though it was my three hundredth time) because I would be seeing it through their eyes. We ate our planned meal and then sat together on the couch with a big blanket. The pause button was absolutely necessary because the girls had a lot of meaningful questions during the movie. We had plenty of time for discussion because phones were not answered and the computers were shut down. This time was special, and it was not interrupted by our typical daily experience.

Movie night and all of the preparation has become a monthly tradition in our house. *The Sound of Music* brought the same amount of pleasure, discussion, and singing as *The Wizard of Oz*. My husband wants to introduce them to his favorite childhood movie, *The Black Stallion*, and my next suggestion is *Mary Poppins*. Really, I don't think the girls care which movie we pick. They are just excited for a time when the energy of the house is calm, happy, and fun and all of the attention is on them. That is what they look forward to, and that is what they will remember.

Disney Plans

Preparing for Disney World was important, but creating a mental plan about how it would go was a mistake. I had assumptions and expectations, and I was surprised when the experience was different. At first I held tight to my expectation of the day and how my children should act, but once I let go and allowed them to be their true selves, the real fun began.

Lesson: Parents often label their children — my shy one, my smart one, my troublemaker. There may be reasons for these labels, but no one word can sum up the many sides of a child. Letting go of the label is like giving your children freedom. Instead of boxing them in, allow them to evolve.

❦

"No, I don't want to go. It's too dark."

My husband and I glance at each other, puzzled. Jacey refuses to go on the Winnie the Pooh ride at Disney World. I remind her that she happily went on the ride two years ago, but she shakes her head and calmly tells us she would rather wait outside with her aunt and infant sister.

Camryn is ready and raring to go. She follows her older sister everywhere, but today she wants to go on the ride without her. She doesn't want to go to bed without her, she doesn't want to play without her, she doesn't even like to ride in the car without her, but at this moment she is willing to have this experience on her own. We are confused by this turn of events.

I know my husband wants to talk Jacey into going on the ride. He wants to convince her that she will like it. He might even try to change her mind by telling her that her *little* sister is not afraid to go. I know he wants to do this because I am contemplating the same thing. While I process what to do, Camryn pulls at my sleeve because she's ready to go stand in line. We scratch our heads. This is not what we planned.

At home we read the Disney Guidebook over and over. We talked about the rides we would go on and how the girls would sit together. Jacey shared her memories of her past Disney experience and promised Camryn she would hold her hand and keep her safe. We created a vision for the day, and here we are struggling with the unexpected.

The pattern continues as Jacey passes on Peter Pan and Snow White while Camryn begs for Pirates of the Caribbean. How can Jacey pass up this opportunity? Doesn't she know the rides are the best part of the trip? Our confusion is doubled by Camryn's sudden desire for independence. Is she really ready for these big rides? Is it okay to let her go without Jacey?

As my husband and I wrestle with these questions, my aunt happens to mention something Jacey said while waiting outside Winnie the Pooh. "Did you know that some people like certain things and some people don't? My mom and dad tell me that I have a choice. I can choose what I like and don't like."

I smile at my husband and we both immediately wake up. We teach our girls to trust themselves, to seek their own personal enjoyment, to not feel obligated to do what everybody else is doing—and yet here we are not supporting their individual expression. We created an expectation for the day, and we weren't allowing for the real moment to emerge. The truth is simple. Today Jacey is not interested in the dark rides, and Camryn is ready to go it alone. It is not what we expected, but *it is what it is.*

It's the end of the day, and the girls decide we should ride *It's a Small World* one more time. We hop in the boat and I watch my two oldest girls hold hands, sing the song, and point to all of sights. I notice that every once in a while they look at each other and smile. I sit behind them, happy to watch their experience rather than create it.

A Letter about Grief: Taking children to a wake or funeral

I wrote this for my friend who lost her mother. She has two young children and she wanted guidance on how to support them. Unfortunately, most families have to deal with a loss at some point. If it is a death, a diagnosis, or a job loss, parents are often unsure how to talk to their children about grief and emotions.

I respect that many different religions and spiritual practices exist. There are also many different belief systems regarding death. Think of this only as a reference— take what works for you and leave what doesn't feel right.

Lesson: *Talk to your children about loss, allow them to ask questions, and support them when they express emotion. Be honest with your children about your feelings and show them that you have the tools to take care of yourself.*

❧

Explain to the children what a wake "is" before you go. What is the purpose, what to expect, who they will see, and so forth. When my Grandma died we explained to the girls that their Grandma's spirit was now with God, but her body still remained. Grandma would look different (at the wake) because her spirit was now with God (heaven, the angels, the universe—use language that they understand). The wake honors her life and allows others to do the same. Her body would then be put in a place where we can continue to honor her (love her, whatever feels right) whenever we choose.

At the wake, let the kids decide where they want to be. If they want to see the body, stand by them and support them. If they don't want to look, that is fine. If they seem to be having a hard time at the wake, be prepared with a backup plan. It might be obvious that they are having a hard time because they are crying or sad, but the sadness could show itself through inappropriate behavior. Just have someone available to take them home or take them for food if necessary.

Ask your kids if they want to go to the funeral after the wake is over. They have now had a chance to experience what it will be like so they can make an informed decision. If they decide they want to go, use the same process—explain what they will see and ask if they have any questions (nothing should be off limits). At the wake and the funeral tell them if they need a break or if they want some time to rest, there will be somewhere to go. Funeral homes and churches usually have comfortable basements. Let them bring a game, a DVD, or a doll— basically anything that gives them comfort and a distraction, just in case they need it.

Regarding emotion

Please know that showing emotion in front of your children is completely healthy and necessary. If you cry and say how sad you are, it gives them permission to do the same. If you hold back or try to be too strong they will be confused and unsure if they can express what they are feeling. It's all right to cry in front of them (today, during the service, or three months from now). Once you have regained composure make sure you talk to them about what they saw. "Mom is so sad about losing Grandma and I am crying because I am going to miss her." Allowing them to see you sad and then pull it together again lets them know that they can cry and then be okay again, too. This is a healthy expression of emotion.

Knowing their parents are sad and seeing them deny their feelings is more traumatizing for children. This can be confusing because they know there is a reason to be sad. They are much more tapped into their emotions and the emotions of others than adults often give them credit for. Find the delicate balance between sharing feelings and respecting the age and comprehension level of your children. Children learn by watching adults process their emotions, but they need to be reminded that adults can take care of themselves. Children should not feel responsible for comforting adults or be put in a position to make adults feel better. This is a burden beyond their maturity level.

Today, tomorrow, and for long into the future, let them know that they can talk to you about anything—if they are feeling confused, if they have any questions, or if they are feeling sad or scared. Children often have a hard time processing death because they often don't have enough experiences to let them know that things will eventually get better. Be open and available for their questions. Comfort them with your hugs and attention.

When they show emotion, allow it. Instead of saying, "don't cry," or "you are fine," try "I am here," or "I hear you," so they know they have permission to let it out. Think of it as their opportunity to release tension—you don't want to stifle it. Once they seem calm you can offer hope. Let them know happy days and normalcy will return again (even though it doesn't feel like it now).

Taking care of YOU

Take care of yourself the best you can and allow yourself to grieve. Don't let people tell you that you only have a certain amount of time to grieve or that you should feel better by a certain date. You need to grieve. It is healthy and if you don't let it out, it will most likely come out some other way (anger, loss of sleep, appetite issues, etc).

Elizabeth Lesser's book, *The Seeker's Guide*, reads:

> Let your grief be as full of joy as it is of sorrow. Let it be proof of how much you've loved, how deeply you've allowed life to live in you, how wide the river of your heart has become. Every experience in which you love and lose is excellent practice for learning to face change and to let go. Instead of turning away from love so as not to invite loss, love fully, and learn to grieve.

Honor this challenging time by feeling it and processing it so you can truly move forward with clarity. Ask for help when you need it—people around you will search for ways to show you how much they care.

The Dance of Life

This experience with Camryn occurred right before this book was set to be published. I wanted to share the story because it demonstrated the importance of talking about feelings, allowing your children to be, accepting the moment, and self awareness. It was the perfect culmination of the preceding lessons — taking the total from 18 to 19 Lessons.

Lesson: Sometimes you just need to be present and hold the space so your children are free to release their feelings. You don't need to tell them what to think or how to feel, you just need to support them and love them. They will do the rest of the work.

∽

The dress rehearsal went great. Even getting ready for the rehearsal went well. My daughter Camryn is usually sensitive to tags and tight-fitting clothing, but she was all smiles as she put on her dress for the dance recital. She needed to wear thick tights, but she pulled them up without frustration. Her hat needed several bobby pins, but she didn't even flinch when I put them in. The whole night flowed flawlessly, which created even more excitement for the actual performance.

On the big night we arrive an hour early to a lot of waiting around. It's hot and the dressing rooms and hallways are filled with people and energy. Boys and girls of all ages are putting on makeup and running around in their costumes. My four-year-old dancer is taking in every moment. About ten minutes before the show parents are asked to take their seats in the auditorium. Camryn stands with her dance group and supervisor and gives me a wave as I walk away to find my seat with the rest of our family.

I sit down and enjoy the opening numbers. I look at the program and notice that Camryn's performance is minutes away. I feel a tap on my shoulder and hear, "Mrs. Adams, Camryn is having a meltdown in the hallway." I hand my one-year-old to my husband and I bolt from my seat to the hallway. I see Camryn there, surrounded by a few girls from her class and a few well-meaning moms. She sees me and begins to cry even harder. I pick her up and she holds onto my neck with all her strength. I am quiet for a minute and then ask what is wrong. She shakes her head and maintains her grip.

I notice that her class is lining up because it is time for them to go backstage. I gently ask her, "Are you going to dance tonight?" She shakes her head no. I make eye contact with her teacher and say, "I don't think Camryn is going to make it tonight." Her teacher says, "Tell her you will buy her something if she gets out there." Another mom chimes in, "Tell her that she *needs* to go out there, tell her she will love it." I hear their words, but I also know their suggestions will be ineffective. I don't think Camryn can see beyond this moment and I can't tell her what to feel.

Her dance group moves backstage and I slowly follow with Camryn clinging to me. I notice lots of oh-no looks from moms and the stage hand seems frustrated that the situation is not resolved. I pull Camryn from my body and say, "Honey, you can dance for a few minutes with your friends and then come back and sit with me. I will stay here and watch you." She shakes her head no and snaps back to hold my neck. I shake my head, close my eyes, and realize that it is time for me to let go. The preceding dance number is now over and Camryn's class is taking hands, ready to go on stage. I take a deep breath and think, *this feels big right now, but this is not important in the big picture. Camryn has loved every dance class for the last six months. She was never motivated by this big moment, she enjoyed the whole process. She loved getting her costume and getting made up. She was so excited to see her grandparents and have dinner with them before the show. She has enjoyed every aspect of this opportunity and not dancing tonight will not take away these experiences.*

I smile a bit, lay my head on her head, and allow these helpful thoughts to float through my mind. Camryn sniffs, looks at me, and lets go of my neck. She jumps down and joins hands with a girl from her class as they walk on stage. She finds her place under the lights and performs through sniffs and smiles. Her performance is even more enthusiastic than the rehearsal. I am absolutely dumbfounded. I look through the curtain and feel dizzy. How did I get from there to here? A mom puts her hand on my shoulder and says, "What did you say to her?" I shake my head and tell her that I said nothing – Camryn simply changed her mind. I find myself crying – maybe because I am relieved or maybe I am overwhelmed by the moment.

After the recital we decide to celebrate by going out for ice cream. I find myself alone with Camryn at a table so I quietly ask her, "Can you tell me what you were feeling right before your performance?" She looks at me and says, "I was just afraid that I would get lost." I sit back in my chair and think, *aren't we all.* Camryn may have been referring to actually getting lost like she did at the museum the week before, or maybe she felt lost because the energy around her was so high. She may have felt lost because her mom seemed far away in the auditorium, or maybe it was simply stage fright because she knew it was a sold out crowd. Whatever the reason, I nod to her and tell her that I understand. I explain that we all feel lost sometimes, even big people. I tell her how proud I am that she decided to walk on that stage even though she was having those strong feelings. I find myself tearing up again because I am moved by her honesty and self understanding.

I too sometimes feel lost as an individual, as a professional, and as a parent. I have moments of uncertainty and fear. I often question whether I am good enough or wonder if I will lose my way. These uncertainties often creep in when I least expect them, so I cherish this new set of tools from my daughter. *Feel your feelings, grab the hands of the people around you, step under the lights, and dance with bravery and joy.*

Conclusion

My daughters are very young so I realize that these lessons are just the beginning. Parenting is a life long job and there is no way to control what happens or predict how everything will turn out. The only thing you can do is focus your attention on the day. Instead of worrying about what did happen or what might happen, give full attention to right now. The only thing we are guaranteed is this moment, so this is where we should spend our energy.

It's not enough to just hope for the best. Be aware of your choices and evaluate if something needs to change. If you are struggling with discipline, educational issues, or self care, take steps towards finding solutions. Find a support network, seek education, and start listening to your gut instincts. Parenting is the most demanding and most important job you will ever have and you deserve to have people that assist and support you.

Take care of yourself so you can role model what it means to have a happy life. Make yourself a priority so you have the presence of mind to be with your children. Give attention to your passions or your hobbies and let your children see you as a whole person with many interests. So many older parents tell me that they wish they could have been happier, more aware, or more present when their children were younger. Learn from their experience. Find ways to practice self care so you can experience the joy of parenting right now.

The parenting years do not have to fly by—you can make a decision to slow down and take it in. Parenting is about really looking at a piece of artwork from preschool, enjoying a book together, and being present enough to have a simple conversation. Your children's experiences today are shaping them into the adults they will become. Inevitably your children will face difficulties and disappointments, but if their life at home is safe and trusting, they can be quite resilient. Resiliency comes from being able to express emotion and having someone who will listen. It comes from knowing that you are loved and that the real you is appreciated and valued. If your children know that you have their back, they can deal with the issues that come their way.

You will have difficult moments and challenging times—this is the natural balance of life. If you can accept this, you will be able to learn from your experiences and move forward. Deciding to walk around with guilt is an energy drain and it does nothing to strengthen you or your family. Appreciate the lessons and use them to evolve rather than stay stuck. If something needs to change, change it. If you need help, ask for it. Children learn by watching how their parents deal with all situations, good and bad.

Visualize yourself twenty years from now with your children. What do you hope to see? What kind of relationship would you like to have? If you hope for happy confident children and healthy relationships, understand that those outcomes depend on today. Practice self awareness so you can have more clarity about your role as parent. Acknowledge lessons so you can continue to grow and expand as an individual. Spend time with your children and listen to them so you know who they are. See the beauty in your children and support them through difficult times. Focus your energy on today so you don't look back with regret about lost time.

My hope is that you begin to recognize the beautiful cycle of parenting. First you take care of yourself so you can better nurture your children. As you nurture your children you learn more about yourself. The more you learn about yourself the better parent you become. This cycle will lead to a more authentic relationship with yourself and a more connected relationship with your children. Enjoy the moments!

Made in the USA
Charleston, SC
16 December 2011